Books by Robert Newton Peck

A Day No Pigs Would Die
Path of Hunters
Millie's Boy
Soup
Fawn
Wild Cat
Bee Tree (poems)
Soup and Me
Hamilton
Hang for Treason
Rabbits and Redcoats
King of Kazoo (a musical)
Trig
Last Sunday
The King's Iron
Patooie
Soup for President
Eagle Fur
Mr. Little
Trig Sees Red
Hub
Trig Goes Ape
Secrets of Successful Fiction (a textbook)
Basket Case
Clunie
Soup's Drum
Soup on Wheels
Justice Lion

Justice Lion

Justice Lion

Robert Newton Peck

Little, Brown and Company

Boston   Toronto

FIRST EDITION

Library of Congress Cataloging in Publication Data

Peck, Robert Newton.
  Justice Lion.

  SUMMARY: Fifteen-year-old Muncie Bolt thinks he's
lost Hem Lion's friendship forever when his father
prosecutes Hem's father for operating a still in Liberty,
VT., during the days of prohibition.
  [1. Friendship—Fiction. 2. City and town life—
Fiction. 3. Prohibition—Fiction. 4 Vermont—Fic-
tion] I. Title.
PZ7.P339Ju   [Fic]   80-24283
ISBN 0-316-69658-7

BP

*Published simultaneously in Canada
by Little, Brown & Company (Canada) Limited*

PRINTED IN THE UNITED STATES OF AMERICA

To Hugh and Jeannette

No man is above the law?

Wrong! All men are above it.

One sweaty little citizen
stands taller than all governments,
all laws, and all kings.

Robert Newton Peck

Justice Lion

Chapter 1 ❧

"Hear them dogs?"

"I hear'em," I said to Hem.

"You know, Muncie . . . I don't guess there's any sweeter music in these here hills than when you can lay down on a quilt of pine and wait for your dogs to bugle a coon."

I felt the brown pineneedles crackle under my back. Folding my hands behind my neck, I closed my eyes; in order to hear Whelper and Blue give chase. Both dogs must have been a good mile off. The sound made me happy that I was with Hem, away up in the hills, smelling all the summer forest night.

"They bumped their snouts into a fresh track. Hope it ain't no possum," Hem said. "And it ain't."

Hemming Lion didn't like to eat possum. Can't say I faulted him too much. To my tongue, squirrel or rabbit baked a less saltier pie. As to eating raccoon, I could take it or leave it. Roast pork with apples beats anything. I helped myself to another deep breath. The air was fresh enough to drink.

"Coon," said Hem Lion, "for sure."

"How can you tell it's a coon, Hem?"

"Easy. Board your eyes real shut and harken tight. Hear it?"

I wanted to fib to Hem Lion that I knew the difference between Blue's yelp and Whelper's. But I really couldn't make out the difference. They might have been chasing a circus elephant for all I heard. What I wouldn't give to learn even half of all the woodlore that

Hem Lion took for granted. I wanted my arm to be as hard as his, and to be as tall. Hem was sixteen, a year older than I was. On top of that, he was Justice Lion's son. Not too many folks in the town of Liberty, Vermont, knew Justice Lion to say hello to the man. Yet plenty of people whispered his name. My wonderings about Justice Lion were cut short when the dogs barked sharper from across the hollow.

"Up the ridge," said Hem, "and circling."

"Will they backtrack?"

"Pa won't own a dog that'll backtrack a scent. So you can be right certain Blue and Whelper won't turn tail. Old Justice would gun a hound that done that. Cut down on him. Leastwise, so he claims, though I never yet seen him do."

"I guess I have plenty to learn about cooning."

Hem Lion shot me a wide grin. In moonlight, his face didn't show the ring of dirt that usually stayed around his mouth after supper. "Muncie Bolt, you be a town boy. So I don't guess I expect you to cotton much to us uproaders and our mountain ways."

"But I'm thankful to learn," I told Hem.

"Good. My ma says that gratefulness is a noble prayer."

"And my father says that most of the things I soak up from you and Uncle Justice could come in handy."

Hem Lion punched my arm. "Your pa's a trustable lawyer, according to old Justice. My old man says an honest lawyer is as common as tits on a boarhog."

"I'll tell Father that. Hem . . ."

"Yup."

"One thing makes me happy."

"What's that?"

"Our dads are both okay. We're lucky."

Hem Lion didn't answer. We just eased ourselves on the pine-needles and looked at the August moon. Closing my eyes, I listened to the distant dogs, trying to decide which one was the up-runner. Was it Whelper or Blue? Except for Hem's slap on a bug, the hounds made the only sound.

"Music," said Hem. "Them two dogs run a coon like a fiddle and a banjo. Pa says it's a tune to jig your heart." His lean body rolled over on one hip and the moon lit up his towhead hair.

Breathing deeply, silently, I let the smell of pine and balsam fill my evening. Inside my cheek was a wintergreen leaf, shiny and stiff. Yet whenever I bit into it, my taste was flooded with flavor. The dogs were more distant now, behind a ridge, or beyond a thicker stand of juniper that muffled their baying. It was my guess that Hem knew where they were, and was confident that both dogs would work the scent without our help. The moment made me smile. Yet I didn't really want a coon to die. A night like this, being with a pal like Hem Lion up here on Kipp's Mountain, always made me want every creature in Vermont to be as happy as I was. Yet I wished the coon would escape.

Hem Lion sighed. His face was handsome, and honest. Much like his sister's. I thought about her every day. Every hour. She was quiet, too.

"What are you thinking about, Hem?"

"Not much. That's the beauty of cooning. The dogs sing to our listening. There's a righteousness to it all. Even to the kill." Hem's voice was hard and a lot deeper than mine. But I was going to answer him.

"I don't agree."

Hem raised up on one elbow. "How so?"

"The dogs," I said. "It sort of spoils the music when I realize that all they want to do is not to tree a coon, but to kill it."

"What did you eat for supper, Muncie?"

The ham that Father and I had eaten came halfway up in my throat. "Meat," I confessed.

Hem grinned. "You, me, and them dogs."

I didn't have to ask what he meant. Maybe this was why I enjoyed my times up in these hills with the Lion family. Father always was saying that no man in Liberty knew more about the Creation than old Justice Lion. And when Hem grew up to manhood, he'd be another Justice, to spawn more.

There were uproaders aplenty in the ridges above the town of Liberty, and a good number were Lions; like Hem and old Justice. And uproad girls like Hem's younger sister, Blessing. I tried not to think too much about Blessing Lion, because I didn't want Hem to guess my feelings. Like me, Blessing was fifteen. Whenever she'd look at me with her doe eyes, brown and soft, I realized that she already knew more than I'd ever hope to know. To me, she seemed so much wiser than the town girls. And sweeter.

I just couldn't bear to have anyone catch me staring at Blessing Lion, knowing that I wanted to wrap my arms around her, hold her close to me. And kiss her in twilight. And I'd have to do it soon or go crazy.

"Dogs and coon," said Hem. "They know."

"Tell me what they know."

"Like they was all Bible-taught," said Hem. "That's what old Justice says, and old Pa gets it right more'n often."

"Dogs and coon?"

"Yup. A coon knows his mission is to run off, or tree, and a coondog is smart enough to sniff and follow. Hark a breath."

We listened. There was no change of tune. The bays of Whelper and Blue echoed through the mountain pines, still in pursuit, each bark bringing them closer to a frightened hunk of fur that both dogs wanted to rip apart.

"Justice calls it Law, and it sure beats any law that all them selectmen pass down in Liberty. You gonna be a lawyer like your daddy?"

"Hem, to tell you truthful, I don't know what I want to become. First a man, then maybe my trade will fruit the tree."

Silently, to myself and to Heaven, I whispered to my own soul: *I want to be a minister*. But this was a private hope. Sort of like my feelings for Blessing Lion. Although I told Hem a lot, these were two thoughts that I held inside, because both were too worthy to be shared.

"What are *you* going to be?"

"Me? Reckon I'll be Hemming Lion."

I smiled at him. He was so fortunate, I thought, to know who he was, what he was. And *why* he was. Clutching a handful of pine-needles, I twisted them, snapping their dryness into fragments, loose ends. Damn! Why does Hem Lion have to be so . . . so sure of life? Like a mountain rose; strong, tough. Father would say resilient. Hem accepts his part of the Creation. Yet where am I?

Where, who, what is Muncie Bolt?

"Yup, I'll be old Hem someday. Old Justice will rise to his reward and Hem Lion will rule the clan. I want ten kids."

"Ten's a lot."

Hem snorted. "Justice sired twenty. Some lit out before I got hatched. His first two women died off. Ma's his third. I got myself cousin and kin thicker than thorn. All through these hills. Lions, Lions, Lions. I get surprised there's enough meadowland for you Bolts and all the rest of the downhillers and townfolk."

"By the time you get done with siring, there won't be." I punched him back.

Hem grinned. "I don't plan to git done."

"Are you sorry you left school, Hem?"

"Nope. Lots about schooling is real sport. Then again, for some-body like me, much of it is one powerful waste of daylight."

"I like school."

"That's because you ain't an uproader. Most kids down in Liberty look at us Lions like they smelled a pig sty."

"I never do."

"Best you don't. Our family's got pride. We aren't on relief, and we don't live off the county, and we don't harm or hurt our neigh-bors. Justice taught us to fear Hell and hoe potatoes, and respect Calvin Coolidge. We laugh and dance and sing a whole bit louder than the shouting Methodists and their down-yonder hymnbooks."

Hem threw a pinecone into the brush.

"Longer," said Hem. "The Lions have been in these Addison County hills before the town of Liberty, so Justice heard tell from his grandpa. Back to Kipp Lion, before Vermont was a state. Kipp Lion and his family were citizens of the English kings. Us Lions got a landgrant. On paper. Justice, he keeps it safeguarded. Rolled in deerskin and inside his strongbox."

"Honest?"

Hem nodded. "I never seed it. But someday it'll be mine, so Justice says. It's a covenant to honor. Signed by a long-ago man, named George Rex."

"Sounds to me like that's a real keepsake, that paper that Uncle Justice holds in his strongbox."

"Justice says different."

"In what way?"

"Pa is always saying that what us Lions best hang onto is the land. Our mountain, not just our hunk of paper."

I nodded. "Father would say Amen to that. Because he believes that true law never has to be written down. It's what all creatures already know. My father says that morality is how living things behave."

Hem Lion sat up quickly. All I could hear was the sudden pounding of my own heart, as I too sat up, to listen to the returning dogs. Whelper and Blue were working our way. Each yowl rang louder than the last.

"Here they come, Muncie. Yup, they're driving that old bull coon right to us. One more minute and we might see him land in our laps. The song of the dogs'll change as soon as the coon gets treed."

Then I heard a new kind of bark. The bugle of a coondog on a clear August night, from a throat beneath a tree, telling every Lion ear on Kipp's Mountain that Blue and Whelper had completed their half of the job.

As we ran, I wanted to ask Hem if I could tote the gun, his battered twenty-gauge; but I guess I knew the answer would be no. Running through a forest after dark with a loaded shotgun was hardly a fitting task for a downhiller; and not for a town boy like me, a lawyer's son. More than that, Hem knew these hills. They were a map in his mind, so he would have to run ahead of me. Knowing this, I believe he wouldn't care too much to have me trailing at his heels, with ready lead.

"Up yonder," said Hem Lion.

"Where?"

With his long arm straight up, Hem pointed upward into a blue spruce. As my eyes sifted through the branches, I saw the two shiny-black beads, and the face of a treed raccoon in the moonlight. At the base of the trunk, Whelper and Blue took turns springing into the air, almost climbing the big spruce tree, tails whipping to and fro in wild excitement. Both coonhounds continued to bugle.

As I saw Hem Lion raise his gun, I near to covered my ears. And closed my eyes, too. I wanted to run.

"Here," said Hem, handing the gun to me. "Ever shoot a coon, Muncie?"

"No."

The gun was heavy in my hands as I sighted upward. Beyond the mouth of the iron barrel, two black little eyes looked at me, judging me. My thumb clicked the hammer back. No, I thought. Gunning a coon up a tree is no measure of manhood. Not of the man I want to be. Do I really want to be another Hem Lion? Isn't being Muncie Bolt enough?

"Hold the gun steady on him, Muncie. Freeze your aim and don't yank the trigger. Just pull her back soft and slow."

Beneath my finger, the curve of the trigger felt hard and cruel. I hated loud noise, and I had heard that a shotgun made more noise than a rifle. Every year, on Memorial Day, I used to almost cry and muff my ears whenever they'd fire off the howitzer in the town square. To honor our fallen soldiers. Well, I decided, it was my turn to honor a coon. Swaying the barrel, making sure I'd miss, I squinted my eyes tight and pulled the trigger.

Wham!

Hem's twenty-gauge kicked my cheek. Real hard. Inside both ears, I heard a persistent ringing that wouldn't quit, as my throat tightened with the sudden explosion of sulphur and saltpeter stinging inside my nostrils. I knew the coon was up in the branches, and alive.

The dogs stilled.

Whelper and Blue looked at me with what I swear was the same expression that Hem Lion wore on his face. A look of disgust, disappointment.

Hem stood with hands on his hips, as though he didn't know what to do or say. Slowly taking the shotgun from my hands, he broke it open, ejected the spent shell that was still smoking, in order to ram in a fresh load. The iron snapped shut.

"Them dogs," said Hem Lion. "If old Whelper and Blue could talk, do ya know what they'd be telling you right off?"

"That I missed."

"In lots of ways," Hem said, "a dog thinks like a man. He expects the other guy to hold up his end, and do proper."

"I'm sorry, Hem."

"Ain't the end of the world." Hem squinted at me. "But ya can't unfair a coondog, Muncie. No more than you can short a neighbor. It's near to robbing a mouse away from a cat. You cheated them dogs, boy. Don't ever think for one breath that an honest coondog won't remember."

Chapter 2 🐦

"Easy now, girl."

Hem Lion rested the gun to the ground. Down on his knees, he stroked Whelper's ears until her whimpering had quieted. Blue still trembled, until Hem held the dog's body close to his chest, running his hand along the shiny, short hair from neck to rump.

"I don't know what to say, Hem."

"Start with telling me true. I want the straight of it, and I want to hear it spoke right out."

"I missed on purpose."

Hem Lion nodded. "For sure."

"You already knew?"

"Yup. Leastwise, I guessed as much. Next time, hand the gun back to me, Munch, and own up to the fact ya don't cotton to the job."

Whenever he called me Munch, as he sometimes did, I knew that Hem wasn't too sore. Besides, his voice was steady and even; totally, coldly in control, as though he had been carved from Vermont marble.

"They'll be other coons," said Hem.

I wanted to say thank you to Hem Lion, yet I couldn't find the right words. Letting out a long sigh, I felt better now that I had the bowels to own up to how I felt about wanting the coon to live.

"Hem, will you tell Uncle Justice?"

"Nope. Enough of us are already in on it. You, me, and a brace of coondogs. Maybe even that hunk of fur up yonder."

We heard a sudden noise from above, a quick swishing of spruce over our heads, causing both Whelper and Blue to stiffen. As they bolted into the brush, a flurry of leaves kicked up behind them. Both dogs sounded again and again.

"Come on, Munch."

"Another coon?"

"Nope," said Hem on the run. "Same one. The old rascal jumped down, for some reason, but dang if I know why. They usual stay treed up."

One thing I could do better than Hem Lion, and that was run. Twisting through the puckerbrush, I was way ahead of him, as his bigger body was toting the shotgun. The coon was nearby, which made me hunger to follow the baying dogs; down a gulley, through a stand of ferns where the air was cool and damp, then up and over a low ridge. Whelper and Blue weren't more than a bark or two ahead of me. A thorn cut my face; yet I didn't slow my pace, not even by a step.

Where we were headed seemed due west, to a new section of Kipp's Mountain where I knew I had never been. No fear of getting myself lost even crossed my mind, because Hem Lion was thrashing behind me, warning me to halt and wait up. No chance of my doing that. I wanted only to beat Hem at something, any-thing, not including a spelling contest. When you're out in front, stay ahead, and don't allow the laggards a glimpse of your heels. Maybe that was what Blue and Whelper were thinking about Hem and me. No, I then thought. Both their minds, and noses, were on a fresh coon track.

"Let'em go, Muncie. Halt up."

But I didn't pull short. If I kept running, Hem Lion would have to give chase.

"Hurry up, Hem," I yelled back over my shoulder.

"No," I heard his voice echo from behind. "Don't go in there, Muncie, hear? Back off."

"How come?"

Hem was winded; his voice yelled to me in spurts of spent breath. "Just because. Ya can't go thataway. . . . Don't know what you're . . . fetching yourself into."

Mire? Quicksand? Horrors of a night forest flashed across my mind. Panthers, or bear? But I'd be safe as long as I trailed the coondogs. Blue and Whelper knew where they were headed, so I'd just shadow them as close as possible, leaving Hem Lion to breathe our dust. I kept running.

A big arm stopped me.

Around my neck, I felt the rough sleeve of a sweaty shirt, and the strong smell of a human that I knew couldn't have been Hem Lion.

"Damn you, boy. I learn you to trespass."

Whoever he was, he had a uproader voice, a slow and singsong twang that always seemed to be unhurried. His arm tightened about my neck to cut off my wind.

"Don't . . . don't . . .," I tried to yell.

"Where you be going is nowheres."

The big arm pinned my head to the trunk of a young tree, holding me fast. Kicking to be free, I tried to holler to Hem, but could not. Hurry up, Hem. Run, before I choke to death.

I heard another voice, "What you got?" It wasn't Hem.

The man who had caught me said, "Don't know. Who are ya, boy? What business you got in the hollow?" His arm eased my neck enough for me to reply.

"I'm Muncie Bolt."

"Who?"

"Muncie Bolt. I live in Liberty."

Two men, both with black beards on their jaws, stared at my face. The second man wore a battered old hat which appeared to be handmade of braided straw.

"You a liar, boy?"

"No . . . no . . ."

"He ain't no Lion," said Straw Hat. He was leaner than Big Arm, high cheekbones, deepset eyes that held a spark of moonlight.

As his face leaned in close to inspect mine, his breath was strong and sour. My nose recognized the tart stench of another man's whiskey, a smell that hung mean and merciless.

Were they Lions? If so, I had never before seen their faces. Strangers, the pair of them. God, where are you, Hem?

"Leave him be."

Both men turned to face Hem Lion. I expected the arm about my neck to ease its pressure; but no, the rough sleeve twisted against my skin. I wanted to throw up. Then the man with the straw hat spoke.

"Best we blind him."

A damp rag of dusty burlap quickly smothered my sight, as a pair of hands knotted the blindfold behind my head. The tightness hurt.

"Back off, Hem."

Hem spoke. "Cousin, he's my friend." There was no panic in Hem Lion's speech, as though he had asked for someone to pass the salt at supper. "And," said Hem, "he's a friend to Justice."

In darkness, at the mention of Justice Lion's name, I felt the bodies of my two captors stiffen. Big Arm let me breathe.

"This skinny tad with you?"

"Yup," said Hem, "with me and the dogs."

"Cooning?"

Hem was quiet. I couldn't see, but I figured he gave the man a nod.

"You ought to reason better, Hem. No sense to fetch a down-hiller to the hollow."

"We was following our dogs, Cousin."

"That all?"

"Yup. This'n be Jesse Bolt's boy. His name is Muncie Bolt and he's known to me and Justice. So's his pa."

"We're takin' him."

"Where?"

"You know where."

No more was said. Blue and Whelper were far off, baying after the raccoon, as I was led through the brushy darkness. The blindfold caused my head to throb.

"Hem?" I said.

"Hush up, boy."

"Gentle him, Cousin," Hem said. "He's no harm to us."

"That ain't yours to decide."

Behind me, at my side, walked the man with the big arms, his fingers hooked into the back of my belt to prevent my darting free or falling. We didn't have far to walk. Ahead of us, more men were talking in low voices, a deep singsong babble of conversation that sifted through the trees.

"Justice?"

Wherever we were, I knew it had to be near a fire. The crackle of wood blended with a sharp smell of smoke. The aroma had a sweet flavor. Turpentine? No, not quite. Also a smell of humanity; hot, sweating men that worked in the night in this hollow of Kipp's Mountain. I heard a voice say the word "sugar." Well, it wasn't maple sap boiling; not in August. And few folks render maplesugar by the dark of the moon.

Whatever it was that Hem Lion's cousins were up to, they didn't rightly cotton to have Muncie Bolt know about it. Or any other downhiller. To my right, I heard whispering; one mountain voice confiding in another. The voices did not sound mean, or cruel. They were merely talking as uproaders talk, a lazy chant that rambles along its lyrical path, between pines, hemlocks, silent cabins of rabbity children who wore meal-sack dresses and no shoes.

My flesh began to perspire.

Gently, but with a firm hand, Big Arm pushed me to the ground where I sat with an abrupt thump. There was no pain intended, or felt. He only seemed to want me to sit and be still. Against the lower half of my face, I felt the fire's heat. Something was burning hot.

"What happens here?"

The question was more of a command, issued by a deep drum of a voice that spewed up and out from a barrel of a chest. The voice could speak more softly than any other man's, because the speaker knew that all present would listen, and obey.

"Uncle Justice," I called out.

As my hands raised to yank off my blindfold, Justice Lion prevented my doing so. It was he who knelt before me, as I knew the way in which he panted, a hoarse and husky wheezing. In August, the big breath of a winter wind.

"No," he said.

"But it's me, Uncle Justice. I'm Jess Bolt's boy. You said I could call you Uncle, remember?"

"I do recall. But I don't guess I expected you here. Not this night."

"I want to take this thing off. I can't see."

"Best you don't, boy," said Justice Lion. "Ain't easy to explain. Wise you don't witness our doings. So stay yourself blinded, boy. Git yourself home and your pa'll tell you the reason I kept you blind."

"But why? Why?"

"We got cause, lad. Your daddy'n' me, us two go back more'n a ways. He'll tell why and you'll be the gladder."

"Uncle Justice, where is Hem?"

"I'm right here, Munch."

Justice Lion said, "Hemming, you done a tomfool thing. Anytime you plan to bring Jesse Bolt's kid or any other downhiller up to the hollow, I got to know in advance. Hear?"

"I hear, Pa."

"You might of got Jess's lamb in deep water."

"Me and Muncie, we had no plan to wander this close to the backwash, Pa. The coon run this way. Dogs followed and we give chase."

"Next time, let the dogs turn free. They'll fetch back when their bellies empty. These be days of troublesome times, this Prohibition. All it done was tempt a man to distrust his neighbor. Hard to tell apart a buyer from a spy."

"Muncie ain't no spy, Pa."

"I agree. But all our family don't witness it thataway. We got kin in the hollow that'll see this here boy as pesky, and do him spite. You want that?"

"No, Pa, I sure don't," said Hemming.

"Me neither." I felt a heavy paw of a hand rest lightly on my shoulder, patting me, telling me not to be afraid. But I was. The crotch of my trousers felt wet against my legs. "Help him up to his feet."

"I will, Pa."

"Stay your friend blind until you can twist him around some and lose his bearing. There you point him downhill, toward Liberty."

"Right away, Pa."

I heard a familiar voice. "No, I don't like it." The voice was that of Straw Hat.

"Festus," said Justice Lion, "you be a free man with rights to speak out. So say it."

The man called Festus, the one in the straw hat, said, "I don't cotton to let this here calf wander off to tattle all he knows. Me an' Arno catched him proper. He ought to get whip-smarted."

"I side with my brother," said Big Arm.

"Aye, and me," spoke another.

"Well now," said Justice Lion, "seems like we's going to stand toe to toe."

"Seems like."

"What's your aim?" asked Justice.

"We make sure he don't report on us."

I heard Justice Lion let out a long sigh. "I know this here boy. I know his pa. And if'n he gives his word, it be good as a bond."

"How do we know that?"

"You knowed it now. I don't guess I plan to sneak tree to tree, or abide in shadows for the rest of my days. Hem, snake off his burlap. I aim to show our good cousins how much of this boy I trust."

"No!" said Big Arm. "He'll run to Rake and snitch."

"Boy, stand up."

I stood. Somewhere, from close by, I felt the presence of a large

17 &

male, a chief, the head of the clans of Lion. Again, the beefy hand found my shoulder.

"What'll I do, Uncle Justice?"

"Just stand mute and let me cogitate. First off, just you answer me straight, Muncie Bolt. I ask you, boy . . . what you have heard this night . . . will you discuss our doings with any living soul, save your father?"

"No, I won't, Uncle Justice. Honest."

"What's more, I now ask you this. Do you have an inkling as to what we men do here in this place?"

I knew. But the best thing to do now was to play dumb. I tried not to smile. "Yes, you're all boiling maple syrup."

Loud and rowdy guffaws burst into the night from all sides of where I stood. I knew darn well why they were concerned about how much I knew. And I figured out that they were stilling whiskey, against the law. Finally their laughing died down.

"Boy," said Justice, "you wouldn't want to sow trouble for us uproaders, would you . . . over a harmless old batch of sap?"

"No, I sure wouldn't."

My trousers felt a wee bit cold between my legs and under my body. Cold and wet, so I bent over some to hide my shame.

"Turn him loose, Justice."

"Yeah. He don't know enough to pour piss out of a boot."

"You all agree?" Justice asked.

"Agreed. But your boy Hemming's got to keep him blind, so he don't never come back. Or show Rake Tatum where we do."

"I'll keep him blind, Pa."

"See to it then. And soon. The boy's in shiver."

"Thank you, Uncle Justice," I told him.

"You thirsty?"

"Yes, sir. And a bit cold."

"Bring the lamb a drink."

I asked them, "Is it maple sap?"

"Not hardly," said Justice Lion.

"What is it?" I asked, as I felt a cool jug thrust against my chest.

"Take a sip. See if you favor it."

Someone's hand jerked out the cork. I reckoned I was about to curse myself with a swig of hard liquor, but I was dead wrong. It was apple-sweet, cool, tart. I swallowed three healthy gulps from the wet jug.

"Hey!" Justice Lion then said. "Easy now, son, or you'll bay at the moon along with them pair o' dogs." The men laughed.

"It's good," I said. "Real good cider. I never tasted cider like this before. How come the jug is so cool and the cider sort of burns hot?"

I heard more laughing. So I asked another question. "It's only August. Cider time's in October."

"Right you be, boy," said Justice. "But this here apple juice set last winter, to harden. I guess it be closer to apple brandy than it be sweet cider."

"May I have another swig?"

"I think nay."

The jug was taken from my hands, and the cork was bunged back to the mouth, but not until I heard a few of the others wet their throats. Inside my gullet, the cider burned brighter than Yule.

"No, my lad," said Uncle Justice. "One full swig is aplenty for your size tumbler. I don't guess I'll send you back to Liberty and to old Jess Bolt with a putrid breath or a dizzy wit. You put your paunch around just enough to spook away a chill from your young bones. Now git."

Hem spun me about, marched me a mile, pulled off the blindfold and headed me down the road toward town. Liberty looked funny, spinning around the way it did. I kept on laughing out loud. But I finally found our house in spite of the fact that I could have sworn that someone moved it.

Our porch boards looked wavy.

Chapter 3 ☙

W ake up, Muncie."
    Hearing my father's voice, I opened one eye, grateful that my wild dream about being chased by black bears, and by men in black beards, was over.

"Father . . ."

"Yes?"

"What time is it?"

"Nearly nine o'clock. I'm on my way to the courthouse to file a deed. Care for some breakfast?"

In my throat, I tasted a sudden rush of last night's applejack. "Yes," I lied to Father.

"Pancake batter is in a bowl next to the stove. Seeing as you were out late hunting with Hem, I decided to let you sleep a few extra hours. Did you boys tree a coon?"

"Sort of."

Sitting up, I rubbed my eyes, then looked at my father who stood with his hands on the brass footboard railing of my bed. He was not a tall man, average or shorter, lean of body and face, hair thinning to near baldness. Unhooking his steelrim eyeglasses from his ears, he polished the lenses with a clean white handkerchief which he then refolded into his pocket.

"You were out rather late?"

Swinging my feet from under the sheet and light blanket, I touched my toes to the bedroom floor. My head spun, throbbing. "I guess you heard me when I came home."

"So I did. You were not overly quiet."

"Sorry. I didn't intend to be inconsiderate. Excuse me, for knocking over the chair."

Father smiled at me. "You're excused, son. I'm glad that you have made yourself a friend of young Hemming Lion. I don't hunt anymore. Guess I don't do much of anything these days, except practice the law. But I most fervently encourage you to savor the woodlands."

"Boy, am I scampered out. Hem and I must have covered ten miles last night."

"Ha. Think how tuckered the dogs must be. If you and Hem did ten miles, the coondogs must have covered twenty."

"Easy."

"There's a cut across your cheek."

"Bramble bush must have gashed me. It don't hurt."

"*Doesn't* hurt."

"Doesn't."

"Hunting with a Lion is one thing, but I do not intend you to employ their uphill grammar."

"I'll try not. The Lions are a lot different from us, aren't they?"

"You notice that?"

"Yes, I do."

Father sat on the foot of my bed. "In what way, would you say, do the Lions differ from people you know here in Liberty?"

"They're wild."

"Indeed. Wild to enjoy their freedom."

"And they sure do that."

"Muncie, the uproaders are like a stand of mountain laurel. Or perhaps more like that thornbush you tangled with. Rough, resilient, resolute . . ."

"I don't think," I said, "that the Lions take to us downhillers a whole lot. Or crave our company."

"True enough. People here in town tend to look down their noses at mountain men. Then, of course, the shoe fits the other foot. Justice Lion holds no truck with Liberty folk. I don't think old

Justice has as much as set one boot in Liberty in more than ten years. Perhaps more."

"He likes you, Father."

"A fact I am proud to honor."

"How come you and Justice Lion are friends?"

"Twenty years ago, I defended his son, Drury. There was a trial in the courthouse, and I got him off."

"What was the indictment?"

Father smiled. "Homicide."

"Wow."

"Accounts of the trial made all the newspapers in Vermont. The State versus Lion."

"Was he guilty? I mean, did Drury Lion really murder somebody?"

"Shame on you, Muncie." My father winked at me. "You know very well that guilt, or innocence, is determined by a jury. Never by gossip. But to answer your question, the prosecution set out to prove, beyond a reasonable doubt, that Drury Lion stabbed a man."

"On purpose?"

"Well, some said during a knife fight."

"How'd it happen?"

"On a Sunday afternoon there was a horse race. Witnesses claimed, at the time, that there had been some heavy betting, plenty of whiskey, which added up to a misunderstanding as to the stakes and a quarrel. Yet the death did not occur until later that evening."

"Who was killed?"

"A man named Al Wheelright."

"Holy cow. Was he stabbed by Drury Lion?"

"Well, some people *claimed* Drury's knife was found protruding from the luckless breast of Mr. Wheelright."

"And you got him off."

"I was fortunate enough to pick the right jury. Henry Gleason was the D.A."

"He's still D.A."

"Yes, old Henry's been the District Attorney for darn near thirty years. At the time, Gleason thought he had an open and shut case. A sure conviction. He went for murder one, asking the jury hang Drury Lion."

"If you stab a man in hot blood, during an argument . . . that's not murder one, is it?"

"No, but you'll recall I told you that the knifing happened later, hours after the quarrel. That, by itself, might constitute premeditation in the opinion of more than one court."

"Do you think Drury Lion really *murdered* him?"

Father squeezed my leg with his thin fingers, digging me just about the knee, making me wince. "Guilt," he said, "is a matter of fact, not of law. If you're sentenced, the State of Vermont will hang you. But your guilt is determined by a jury, not by a judge or by a law."

"And the jury acquitted him."

Father said, "So they did."

"How did you do it?"

"I picked the right jury."

"Were they all Lions?"

My father laughed. "Mercy, no. Henry Gleason never would have held still for such a caper. Each member of a jury must be approved by both attorneys, prosecution and defense."

"Did you select people that were friendly toward the Lions?"

"No, I did not. Besides, friends of the Lions would be a bit hard to find. At least here in Liberty. Yet there *are* some."

"Then who'd ya pick?"

"Out of the twelve jurors that we chose, I picked one man who I knew hated Allen Wheelright."

"Cleve-."

"During an election, Muncie, I have observed that citizens vote a grudge more often than a loyalty."

"So you reckoned that one juryman would vote in the same way."

Father nodded. "One is all you need."

23 ❦

"You really love to practice the law, don't you?"

"That I do, son. It's sort of like a game of chess, or checkers, or even poker."

"Like poker?"

"In a way. You never win a pot by leaning forward. So tilt back your chair, breast your cards, hang onto your guts . . . and wager."

"You used to play poker, didn't you?"

"Yes, at one time. Before your mother died, I would play one evening a week. Friday nights. As a matter of record, we often played at Henry Gleason's, because Friday was the evening that his wife, Mabel, attended choir practice at the Methodist Church."

"How come you quit playing poker?"

"Muncie, when we lost your mother, a long time went by before I did anything at all. Not even shave."

"I remember that."

"You were only five."

"But I remember how rough your face was whenever I hugged you, and cried."

"I envied you, Muncie."

"How so?"

"An envy for your tears, I mean. When your mother passed on, for some reason I just couldn't cry. Because everything stopped. Every gland in my body was empty. Drained dry. As you know, it took us both a lot of years to regain our footing."

As my father spoke, both of us looked at the picture of my mother, held in a silver frame, which always rested on my bureau. Her hair had been a soft brown, waving gently back to pin in a bun. The photograph was in black and white, yet I remembered how her eyes sparkled with blue. Her face had been slightly freckled, the way you sometimes see a yellow apple, with a modest blush of pink.

My father sighed. "I'm not over it yet."

"No. I don't guess we ever will be. But I sort of wish you'd play poker some week. The way you once did."

"Never again."

"Why not?"

"Because, my lad, your mother never really approved of poker. Thus I played the game openly, before she died, more to tease her than to fan the cards. Call me a member of the old school, but now that Laura is gone, ironically I am no longer free to play."

I socked him easy. "You're a dear old dad."

"Am I?"

"You bet you are. For my dough, you're the best father in the whole doggone universe."

"Well, I try to be. And often fail."

His face shot me a joyless smile. The expression he wore made me want him to engage in some sort of fun, to do things that he enjoyed. Jesse Bolt did not hunt, fish, play poker, attend church, or venture beyond our dooryard in the evening. On our front porch we kept two rocking chairs. He would often occupy one of them, on a warm summer evening. Then, when he thought no one was observing, he'd reach over to touch the arm of the other chair, to rock it slowly back and forward in rhythm with his own.

"I'd never want any sire except you."

Father smiled. "Half a family. I guess that's what you and I add up to. Yet we're a good team, aren't we?"

"The best."

"Now then, the grass looks to be cut. Soon as your breakfast gets eaten, best you follow the lawnmower. Mrs. Bly will be coming in to clean any minute, so stay out from under her feet. And please weed the flower beds by the frontstoop."

"Today?"

"Of course. What's wrong with today?"

"Nothing. Except that I'm a bit wore down from cooning."

"Son, I'll tell you something about poker and coonhunting. Evening pleasure should not rightfully interfere with the following day's labor. Not my poker, nor your ramming around a mountain."

I yawned.

Quickly my father scowled, causing me to wonder what displeased him so abruptly. I didn't have to ask.

"Your breath."

I tried to grin but it didn't spread naturally on my face. I was forcing a smile which didn't fool my father. Well, I might as well own up.

"Hem had some cider."

"I presume that to mean that both of you took a pull on a jug."

I nodded. "I had three sips. That's all. It was applejack. Darn near burned out my bowels a second after I swallowed it down. Sure wasn't October cider."

"Ah, then the bending over to pluck dandelions from a flower bed appears to be less appealing than usual."

"Sure does."

"Well, if you dance, Muncie, you have to pay the fiddler. No one forced you to drink it."

"No, I don't guess they did. I was a bit on the wet and chilly side, so I figured a slug or two for medicinal reasons would ward off a misery. I can't abide to take cold or run a fever."

Father nodded. "I'll buy that. You're fifteen. Man enough to swill some applejack if you so reason. Such a decision is yours to make, because it's your gullet, your headache, and . . . I'm not at all reluctant to repeat . . . your flower bed."

"Fair enough. I'll pay the fiddler."

"I try not to nag you, Muncie. Do I?"

"You don't a whole lot. I guess applejack carries its own penalty, without your adding to the sentence."

"Well spoken." Father's hand reached forward to tousle my hair; but stopped, as I guessed that he knew my head would not be welcoming much rough and tumble treatment. Not this morning.

I stood up. Headache and all, I wasn't going to give in to my shoddy feelings, even though pulling off my pajama shirt didn't exactly feel so hot.

"Did you ever drink corn whiskey?" I asked Father.

"A few times. Why?"

"No reason. I was just wondering."

"If you think hard applejack cider has a kick to it, boy, I suggest you reserve your sampling of white whiskey to later years. And for only special occasions."

"Makes sense," I said.

Frowning slightly, my father said, "You saw something last evening, didn't you. Someone up on Kipp's Mountain engaged in what can oft be referred to as moonlight farming?"

Jesse Bolt never failed to amaze me. Not that he followed me around, spying on me; yet what he knew of my activities could ink up a journal. I guess my face was now telling him that he'd once again hit the bullseye.

"I didn't see for sure."

"Best you don't. Mind your own business, Muncie, and stilling corn whiskey is certainly none of your affair. Forget what you saw, repeat it to no one; not even to me and especially not to Hem Lion. Most important, skirt the place where you saw nocturnal activity. Avoid it."

"How come you got so serious all of a sudden?"

Father faced me squarely. "Muncie, crime is always a serious matter. Thanks to the thoughtless in Washington and in Montpelier, and the Bureau of Prohibition, the law sorrowfully claims that a man no longer has a right to cook a run of whiskey."

"You don't agree?"

"Hell, *no,* I don't agree. If we are to remain free men in these United States, we ought to spurn such tomfool restrictions on a man's liberty. Next thing you know, Congress will pass a law that says we're not allowed to eat turnips, play poker, sing in church, pray to Heaven . . . or even breathe."

"How come they made Prohibition a law?"

"Fools did it. You can't legislate good conduct. Besides, I know a lot of souls who still up corn, and they are some of the most moral and Christian men on Earth."

Chapter 4 ❧

"H owdo."

As her voice roared, Petunia Bly banged the screen door, entering our kitchen where I was forcing down my third and final pancake. The long wooden handle of her mop whanged against the cylindrical hot-water tank that was part of the big, black, Acme-American cookstove, causing my head to throb.

"It's nine o'clock, youngster. Half a day near gone and you ain't yet fed your face?" Mrs. Bly asked me in a voice that could have been clearly heard for a mile upwind.

"Morning, Mrs. Bly."

"Hah! Morning was three hours ago."

With a big and beefy arm, Petunia Bly raised her scrubbucket, setting it down heavily on the table where I was eating. Her every action, every word, spoke a disapproving jar to my ailing head.

"Where's your pa?"

"He went to the courthouse to file a deed."

"A decent man, Jesse Bolt. If'n you ask me, he's plumb wasted."

"Wasted?"

Mrs. Bly brandished her mop as if she gave her inner thoughts a command to charge. "Ain't right. Mr. Bolt ought to be married. I can't reason why such a good catch ain't been caught."

Her every word was a scream, as if her purpose was to hammer a railroad spike into each of my ears. I wasn't interested in her opinions. Nor in her volume. Yet I couldn't help smiling at Petunia

Bly, because I knew she liked Father. Over the years, he had helped her over a few rough spots, and she was one more Vermonter who would always be grateful.

"How come you slept so late?"

"Father failed to wake me."

"Huh." Mrs. Bly clunked the scrubbucket into the sink. "If'n you was *my* boy, you'd a been up at six, like honest folks, else I'd a booted your butt from Hell to supper."

"Yes'm."

"Saturday's a work day."

I nodded grimly, thinking about the flower beds and the lawn-mower.

"There's talk," hollered Mrs. Bly.

"Talk?"

"Yup." She threw a big brown cake of Octagon soap into the filling bucket. "Over at the mill, there's talk about the men all puttin' in a five-day week."

"There is?"

"Sinful. I'm near to fifty, and I never worked no five-day week. What's more, I couldn't name one woman in Vermont who ever did. Five-day week. What'll they fix to do on Saturday? Hang around at the poolhall, if you want my opinion."

I didn't want Petunia Bly's opinion, yet there were few citizens in Liberty who couldn't hear it.

Mrs. Bly eyed my plate. "You through?"

"Almost. I have to go outside and cut the grass. And weed. By the way, how's Jack?"

"Better. Doc says he's a strong kid and the stitches'll mend rapid. Beulah takes care of him proper. Larkin and Chester got into a fist-ing over a sweet potato. Tess says she'll leave home. She won't. Harmon teases her a mite some. But then, when he was the young-est, he got the britches twist off him by Halo and Clemson. And the other one, Eunice."

"They'll turn out, Mrs. Bly. That's what my father always pre-dicts."

"Best they do or I'll gut their gizzards. Between me and the Methodist Church, maybe half'll amount to something." Water sloshed on the kitchen floor as if caused by some unseen Divine tide.

"I figure, Muncie, if I fear the Lord and raise'em right, they'll poop or prosper. Harry ain't a whale of a help to me." She smiled a broad grin on her pink moon of a face. "Yet at least I got me a husband. He don't make the living. But when the lights go out, he makes the living worthwhile."

Mrs. Bly always made me laugh. You couldn't be human and not appreciate her. Father said the same. More than once we had found former rips in our clothing that Petunia Bly had mended and said nothing about. If the town of Liberty had a mother, she was it.

"Now git!" she ordered me. "A kid in a kitchen is worse'n three cats. I oughta know. Us Blys got five cats and half of 'em's pregnant."

I laughed. "Well, it's good to know our town is growing."

"Out."

"I'm going."

"Hey, it's hot in the sun. Come inside before noontime and I'll pour you some cold buttermilk."

"I don't think we have any."

"I brung some."

"Thanks."

"Git. Less you want my ire."

"Not today."

Outside, the summer sun of morning made me squint. Looking down at the grass, I could see that it was already higher than a lawn demanded. Letting out a deep sigh, I pulled off my shirt, hanging it on a bent nail just outside our toolshed. I opened the door.

The hinge squeaked.

Inside, the toolshed was dark and damp. One of the panes in the window had been knocked out and never repaired. As I reached for the mower, a long strand of spiderweb stretched across my face. Against the dim light from the dusty window, I saw a large gray spider near the center of the web. She was a mare, I concluded from over a score of tiny spiderlets about her. I wondered if she would ever eat her own young.

"Hey there, spider."

Touching the hub of her web with the tip of my finger caused her to scamper along a silvery strut into a window corner. Well, I reasoned, at least her web would prevent the hornets from nesting in the shed. I removed the mower as carefully as possible in order not to destroy her web.

"Did you ever drink hard cider?" I asked the spider. "Well, don't do it. It may be sweet on Friday night, but it sure can turn a body sour on Saturday morning."

We had a front yard and a back yard; in all, about two-thirds of an acre of land, according to Father. Cutting it once a week was about a two-hour job. The spinner sent a fountain of green clippings showering up into the front of my trouserlegs. I sneezed more than once, and it always made my eyes itch. Maybe I had a touch of what people called hay fever.

I mowed the entire lawn, and swept off the front walk, hung up the broom, bristles-up, between two pegs, and started to tackle the weeding.

"Here ya go!"

Petunia Bly handed me a generous tumbler of buttermilk. In my throat it was cool and sour, yet I wondered how well it would mix with applejack and pancakes. I handed the sorry-looking glass back to Mrs. Bly.

"Thanks," I said. "It's real tasty."

"You don't look too peppy to me." Her hand felt my brow. "Are ya sure you ain't come down with a fever?"

"Reckon I'm just hot from mowing the lawn."

"Stick out your tongue."

"What for?"

"Don't sass me, Muncie. Stick it out!"

Making the meanest face that I possibly could, I stuck my tongue out at Petunia Bly.

"You're a caution." She laughed.

"Satisfied?"

"Your tongue's coated."

"Well," I said, "what did you expect to see on a tongue that just gulped down a whole glass of buttermilk?"

"Hmpf. I s'pose you got a point." Her red hand tilted my head back until I was blinking into noon sun. "Your eyes look a bit on the rosy side."

"Hay fever. From the grass."

"Did you scrub your teeth after you ett your breakfast?"

"No. Guess I forgot."

"Best you don't forget again. Muncie Bolt, you got the breath of a sick goat."

"It's the buttermilk."

"Not likely. You'd blame the World War on buttermilk if'n I'd let ya get away with it."

Mrs. Bly stood by the sink while I scrubbed my teeth. She was right. A clean mouth made me feel a bit brighter.

"There," she said, "that's more like it. I heard tell that President Harding brushed his teeth three times a day. And some say that's all he ever did, rest his soul."

"I don't want to be President."

"You don't, eh? That's it, slush the water around in your mouth real thorough, until you can count up to twenty. Then spit."

I spat.

"Rinse out the basin, hear?"

"Yes'm."

As I ran the tapwater, I wondered why Father and I worked for Petunia Bly. But I didn't say it.

"You don't get elected President of the United States with a dirty mouth."

"No," I said, "I don't guess you do. Anyhow, I'm not planning on being the President. Leastwise, not today."

"Don't get fresh."

Pinching my ear, drawing me close to her, she kissed the top of my head. I was sort of pleased that she did it. There were moments in my life that I wanted to put my arms around Mrs. Bly and hug her real hard. Not that I wanted her to be my mother or anything like that. Yet she was just somebody worth a hug now and then, sort of the way you say howdy to folks on the street, or stop to pet a stray cat. Even though she was closer to the size of a horse.

I liked the way Mrs. Bly always smelled, of soap and hard work. I told that to Father once and he said that Petunia Bly was a fragrance all her own, a blend of sweat and sweetness, spiced with a dash of vinegar, a dish to serve the empty.

"Flower beds need weeding."

"Yes'm. I'm fixing to do it."

"When? On Christmas?"

"No," I sighed. "Right away."

"You looked peaked to me. Sort of pale."

"Oh, I can explain that, Mrs. Bly."

"Well . . ."

"It's the buttermilk."

An inch ahead of her boot, I raced out the door. My head was still pounding, but at least my mouth felt a whole lot fresher, preparing me to attack the flower beds with a more willing heart. Inside the house, I heard Mrs. Bly pretending to call me a whole string of no-account names, discussing my impertinent manner with her bucket and brush.

Less than a minute later, an upstairs window flew open, where she vigorously shook a throw-rug at me with silent contempt. Father often stated that in all of Vermont, Saturn, and the Milky Way, there could be only one Petunia Bly.

One was enough. Because on a day like today I could not have stood two.

"Weeds," I said.

Looking down, I saw the blooms of dandelions shining up at me; each blossom was orange in the center, softening to a yellow around the outer edge. A bee worked one of them, then flew off to a clump of clover beyond our fence. Picking a dandelion, I let the milk of the stem ooze out into a tiny white doughnut. I tasted the bitter taste, wondering how cows in the meadow could stomach such a variety of vegetation and remain so content.

Turnips were bad enough.

A sound scratched my ear. Boots, scraping along on the sidewalk in front of our house, steps moving from one square to the next, along slates that varied in color . . . blue, purple, lavender, blue-gray, and a deep charcoal. Without looking up, I recognized the person who approached with his determined limp. To my knowing, only one soul in the town of Liberty walked with such a pronounced and uneven shuffle. Sometimes, not quite asleep at night, I heard him walk our street. Only in summertime through my bedroom screen.

"Good morning, Muncie."

"Oh, howdy there, Mr. Tatum."

Looking up from my bended-knee position, I smiled at our bypasser. He stopped. Sheriff Rake Tatum was about my father's age, possibly older. Father said that he was a man with no enemies and no friends. Each election, every two years, Mr. Tatum was opposed. But never defeated. People in Liberty, and all over Addison County, voted for Rake Tatum, with a regularity equal to milking.

"Weeding, I see."

"Yes, sir, I sure am."

"Place looks prim."

"Thank you."

"Your pa to home?"

"No, he sure isn't. About nine o'clock, he took over to the courthouse to file a deed."

As I spoke, Mrs. Bly must have bumped the carpet-sweeper into a chair. Rake Tatum's eyes left mine as he looked at our house, not calling me a liar. Yet with a law officer's curiosity.

I said, "Mrs. Bly's inside, cleaning."

"Never said she wasn't."

I guess I knew why Sheriff Tatum wore his badge for so many years. Father once said that Rake Tatum in his own quiet way could limp faster than most of our local scoundrels could run. That was when I had asked my father if he voted for Mr. Tatum whenever he ran for sheriff.

"Always," he'd said.

"Well," I said, "are you catching many lawbreakers these days, Sheriff?"

Rake Tatum spat. "Only the bad ones."

The way he said it made me think about the Lions up on Kipp's Mountain, stilling whiskey. I wondered what Sheriff Tatum thought about Justice Lion and his uphill clan. For sure, I wasn't going to mention what I'd stumbled into last night, because I didn't want misfortune to visit the Lions; not to Hem, Blessing, or Uncle Justice. Thinking about which side of the law people were on sort of made the buttermilk churn inside my stomach.

"It's the times, boy."

Wow, did Rake Tatum know what I was wondering about? Nobody could be that smart. Except for Father.

I asked, "You mean Prohibition?"

Rake Tatum spat again, into the dust of the road, brown beads of tobacco juice that to look at didn't help my ailing digestion a whole lot. "Yup. Some folks want it. Others don't. And to tell you the straight of it, Muncie, this Prohibition business can plant down a law officer right betwixt a rock and a hard place."

"Father says between the Devil and the deep blue sea."

"I'm in there somewhere, I reckon." Mr. Tatum's hand raised to touch the metal badge that was pinned to his shirt. "A star points in several directions, all to once. It don't point in just one, like a bird dog."

"Which point do you follow?"

Shifting his cud of Red Man chewing tobacco to a fresh cheek, Rake Tatum squinted at me, removing his haymaker hat that was a 59-center pressed out of straw. His hat was cowboy style, but his mule-ear boots were regular Vermont.

"Which point do I follow? A thorny question. But I don't guess I'd have to cogitate much to answer."

I waited. His fingertip lightly touched the starpoint that was straight up.

"Hopefully, the one that points to the Almighty."

Cane in hand, Rake Tatum limped away, heading in the general direction of the courthouse.

Chapter 5 ❧

From where I sat on a protruding hunk of rough granite, I could look down through green treetops and see the entire village of Liberty.

Almost all the houses were white, flanked by red barns, or outbuildings of whitewash. Plenty of the hay barns had seasoned to gray and, to my eye, looked as though they would stand for always. Father once said that Vermont barns were akin to Vermont farmers, strong in the beam, built to face up to winter. I had sort of reasoned it all out in my own mind that Jesse Bolt was proud to be a lawyer; yet still prouder to be a citizen of Vermont.

Up through the green leaves of summer, the spires of the Congregational and Methodist churches reached up toward Heaven, or at least to scratch the sky. Twin lances of dueling knights, saluting one another, prior to combat. Yet the lances never crossed. Year after year, both flocks seemed to share the pasture without conflict. Reverend Murphy and Reverend Waller went fishing together, but, my father said, not in each other's pond.

"Hello down there," I said, to no one in particular. I just sort of felt like yelling to my home town, to let them know that I wasn't up here on the mountain to be a spy. Just a friend.

Leaving the lip of rock upon which I'd been resting, I climbed higher, up through a stand of cool pines, hearing the dry crackling of fallen needles whisper beneath every step. My head felt clearer. Father said that when it comes to morning medicine, work is more potent than pity or piety. And I was sure that Petunia Bly would have salted such a statement with one of her judicial nods.

"Muncie?"

Hearing my name made me jump. The surprise of it was a wild, electric feeling that whip-snapped my spine. My head spun left, then right, searching for the person who had called me by name.

"Over here."

Turning, I saw Blessing Lion.

"Howdy," I said. Wow! I felt happy.

She stood among the upper lace of tall ferns; her brown eyes, the color of forest earth, staring at me. Her dress of pale green appeared to have been woven from the stems of leaves, and as she took her first step toward me, I saw that she was barefoot. Inside my chest, my heart was roaring, "Blessing Lion! Blessing Lion!" so strongly that I feared she would also hear. My hands raised to muffle my shirt.

"You looking for Hem?"

"No," I said. "I'm looking at you."

"At me?"

"Yes'm."

"You all by your lonesome?"

"Yes, I'm alone. Are you?"

Blessing nodded. The pale green dress was not at all new, and as she slowly stepped closer to where I stood, I could see how she had seemed to mature since the end of school. The dress was too snug to hold her breasts, too short to cover all of her thighs; yet Blessing had the modesty of a young woman who is no longer a girl.

Did I look like a man to her? My lungs filled with piny air as the muscles of my legs suddenly grew hard.

"I don't guess," she said, "there's nobody here on the ridge but us two."

Her voice made me swallow. A fool's gesture, because my mouth felt so very dry, as though I could spit cotton.

"Just us two," I said.

"My brother likes you, Muncie Bolt, and he told me so this morning."

Blessing Lion sure knew what to say to make me feel easy. I smiled at her with all of my face and she smiled back. With a soft flutter of her hand, she pulled a maple leaf from a young tree, twisting the stem between her delicate fingers, allowing the leaf its own merry waltz.

"You're watching me, Muncie."

"I know. Can't help it. I watch you in the schoolroom every day. Almost every minute."

"Why?"

"Because you're so fair I can't stop."

Saying nothing, her eyes fell to the leaf that spun slowly in her hands. Her mouth opened as if to answer, but no words came. Only silence, and treetop birds. Behind her, the distant drum of a partridge caused her to look up at me, smiling.

"I try to not look at you," she said, "very much."

"How come? Because I'm ugly."

Her laughter took flight, a forest wren that suddenly wafted away into the trees and was gone, into a darkening sky.

"No. It's 'cause I yearn to."

"That makes me real happy. To know that you want to watch me. I don't guess I know a whole lot about gals."

"We're growing up. Sometimes I long to grow up to be a woman. And then, other times, I just want to be a girl forever. Like in a sweet dream."

"I know."

Seating herself on a fallen log, Blessing Lion looked up at the sky, and I could see the cream of her throat, just beneath her chin. I sat down beside her on the log, feeling my hands shake; hearing my heart beat as again and again it pumped her name into my ears. She looked at me.

"You ever kiss a girl?"

I wanted to run. But as my body seemed to be suddenly poured into fresh cement, I couldn't move. All I could manage was to look at her leaf.

"Me? Not a whole lot."

"Ever?"

"No."

"Do you want to?"

As she spoke, her maple leaf reached upward to touch my face, making me close my eyes for only a breath as the tips of its fingers found my ear.

"Yes, I want to very much."

As sunlight touched her hair, so did my hand, caressing the cornsilky softness, feeling as though I was making some sort of magical discovery. Turning her face, her mouth sought my hand, kissing it lightly with kiss after kiss.

"Never," she said. "Not in my whole life have I ever kissed a boy. Until now."

"Thank you." As I said it, my two words sounded so stupid. Not at all like what a man ought to say. Boy, I thought, am I ever a dumb kid.

"Your neck's got a sunburn, in back."

"I was mowing the grass this morning."

Blessing's fingers touched the back of my neck, beneath my hair. Her touch was light, as though she was afraid; yet I knew that the Lions were never frightened of very much in this world.

"Does it sore?"

"No," I said. "Not the way you touch."

"I never touched you before. Except at school, years back, when we used to join hands and make a circle."

"I remember. That circle game we played."

My hand stroked her hair. And I could read the pleasure on her face. Her eyes closed. "Cats are lucky," she said. "A cat gets herself petted all the time."

"Would you like to be one?"

Blessing nodded. "Yes, if I was your cat."

"That's funny."

"What is?"

"Well, I was thinking that I'm starting to feel like a dog, a happy old coonhound that's fixing to bark at the moon. And hunt and chase and tree."

She laughed. "I'll be a cat. You be a dog."

"Trouble is, I don't want to be a dog. Right now, I want to be a grown man. I want to be Mr. Muncie Bolt."

"And I'll be Miss Blessing Lion, so you can come courting."

"Guess we're courting right now."

"Then let's have at it."

Leaning toward me, Blessing's eyes slowly closed as her mouth came to mine, with lips that were soft and warm and wet. Not knowing quite what to do with my hands, I didn't do much of anything. Together, our mouths moved slightly, as if we were trying to devour some delicious dessert. I smelled her smell and tasted her taste. Blessing Lion. I'm kissing Blessing Lion and she's kissing me! I couldn't stop, as though her face was all candy. So I kissed her cheeks and eyes and hair. I did everything but breathe.

Jumping up, I yelled "Whoopee!"

Rolling over and over on a brown bed of pineneedles, I kicked my feet up at the sunlight, throwing a pinecone into the air.

"What's the trouble?"

"I kissed you. Yup, I finally got up the guts to kiss you, Blessing Lion, and I sure hope this means you're my girl."

Panting, lying on my back with arms and legs extended, I felt like a crazy star. I wanted to sing and dance, shed off all my clothes and run naked through the woods and never feel the prick of even one thorn. Eyes closed, I drew in a deep breath, to let it gently escape.

"I like your name. It's right joyous to say Muncie Bolt."

Blessing lay down beside me, to again whisper my name into my ear. "And I kissed Muncie Bolt. I'm going to kiss you again."

Arms around each other, our bodies warmly pressed together, we hugged and kissed and laughed. Her mouth was soft and free, flying over my face as though her lips had wings.

"You are a beautiful boy."

"Me?"

"All the girls at school want to kiss you."

"Gee, I wish I'd known that."

Blessing pinched me until I winced. "They'd best not kiss *my* boy."

I was lying on my back with Blessing above me, her two legs holding one of mine. As her face looked down at me, hair the color of honey framed the picture of her face. She had cow's eyes, soft and brown and very gentle. Very female.

"Your face is so sweet, Muncie Bolt, but your eyes are so hard. They look deep inside me, so deep into me that I'm near feared of you."

While staring at her eyes, my hands covered her breasts, causing her mouth to open. Slowly she bit her lower lip. Her dress had somehow loosened, allowing my hands to move freely beneath her breasts. When I stopped, she moved her body against my hands, teasing my open palms with her nipples.

"Am I sinful?" she said.

"No. Neither am I. Because I couldn't ever have a sinful thought about you, about any of you, or all of your body. If I saw you naked, I'd feel . . ."

"How?"

"I'd feel cleaner than holy."

"I know. That's why I want you to see me."

"With no clothes on?" I couldn't believe that I was really saying the words to her, out loud.

Blessing bit her lip again. "Yes."

"When?"

"Right now."

Raising herself up from me, she pulled up her dress, very slowly, pulling up the pale green and faded cloth until her legs were naked. "Look at my legs, Muncie. I want to watch your face while my dress is coming off."

I almost screamed.

"Touch my legs, Muncie. You can rub me raw if you want to. I want you to see my body and touch me and kiss my belly . . . and my breasts. I feel so pinky."

I touched her gently. "You feel pious."

"I love the summertime. My body feels so warm. Ripe as corn. Do yours?"

Blessing Lion's hands loosened the top button of my shirt. "Yes," I said. "I never felt so warm before. It's like I'm baking into a butter biscuit."

"I want to kiss your chest." Inside my shirt, her hands explored, fingernails clawing into my skin, biting me like ten little mouths, stinging harder than hornets. Lowering her head, her hair teased to and fro along my chest. I heard thunder in the sky.

"You'll . . ."

Blessing said, "I'll what?"

"If we keep up you'll have a baby."

"Do you want me to, Muncie? Is that what you want to do . . . put a baby into me?"

"Oh, God, I don't know."

"I'm so scared I'm shaking."

"So am I. But I've thought about being with you so much."

"Are you going to put your baby into me?"

"Do you want me to?"

Pulling her dress up and over her head, Blessing was astride my chest, and all bare. She wore no undies. "Muncie, I'm so frightened. I feel so hot, like there's no air to breathe."

"I'm hot, too."

"And I'm scared about a baby."

"So am I. But maybe we're not old enough to be a mother and father."

She lay down close to me again, gripping me with both arms, both legs; her lips lightly touching my mouth. "We're old enough. I think about kissing you all the time. Every minute. The way I hope you think about me."

"You do?"

She nodded. "In my bed at night, before falling off to sleep, I always put my arms around my pillow and . . ."

"And do what?"

"I pretend it's you. Sometimes I even put my legs around the pillow and wish real hard."

"Wow."

"Here, I show you. Like this. Pretend you're my pillow." She rolled over to lie on her side, close to me. "Now I've got my arms around you and my legs around you, and I wish . . ."

"Gosh, I'm scared."

"Me, too."

"Blessing, I'm so doggone scared that I can't even think. All I can do is feel. Your body feels so pretty. I want a hundred hands so I can touch you everywhere at once."

Against my face, I could feel the wetness of her tears. Or were they mine? Father had said that it was wrong to take pleasure at the expense of someone else's pain . . . and it hurts to have a baby. Mrs. Bly even said so. I figured that Mrs. Bly knew enough to be some sort of an expert.

"Oh, Muncie . . ."

Blessing was sobbing, crying against my face as if her heart was near to breaking. I don't want to hurt you, Blessing. I want to love you. Forever, always, until I die. How could love be so hurtful? I can't put my baby into Blessing Lion. But I want to. Am I going to explode? Blow up?

"Muncie . . . Muncie . . ."

Her voice was soft, feeble and frail, weaker than the mew of a blind kitten trying to crawl to its mother's milk. Whatever else happens, I promised myself, I'm never going to hurt Blessing.

Thunder! Louder this time.

Clinging to Blessing Lion, I suddenly felt the tap of a single rain-drop upon my cheekbone. Another, into my ear. Rain. It came faster and harder, driving against my face and body until Blessing and I lay holding each other in a torrent. Wet hair clung to my face, her hair and mine. And in my arms, her body cooled sleek and slippery. Slowly her legs relaxed until she was laughing, kissing my face, fingers entwined into my hair.

"Muncie, I'm so thankful for you."

"There's so much for me to tell you, but I can't seem to think of anything. Except that it's a warm rain, we're both soaking wet, and I don't give a rat's rump . . . except that I'm awful happy. And I'm glad we won't have to worry about . . . a baby."

"Muncie, are we in love?"

"Reckon so. And if your brother ever caught us together like this, he'd bust me proper. And you, too. Even though nothing happened."

"Let me button your shirt."

"Best you put your dress on first."

"How does folks ever put on a wet dress?" She snaked into it, somehow, rolling the darkened cloth down over her wet body. It was still raining. Yet we stood in the rain, hugging each other, laughing.

"You're a man, Muncie Bolt."

"Are you sure about that?"

Blessing kissed my wet face. "I can tell."

Chapter 6 &

Blessing held my hand.

We had walked through the woods together, soaking wet, for about a mile or so. Sometimes at a trot. Then we paused to take a breather. Her arm pointed off to the right, as her free hand covered my mouth, as if to keep me quiet.

"Shush," she whispered.

"What is it?" I managed to say between the gaps of her fingers.

"Look over yonder."

Keeping low, Blessing and I moved behind a long row of wet juniper bushes that sprouted from a long split in a rock. I still didn't see anyone or anything. Then I heard a noise, like a mallet hitting a metal barrel. And I saw a slim curl of gray.

"Smoke," I whispered.

"It's from the furnace."

"I know what they're doing, I bet."

"Well," she said, "seeing as you do, best you keep righteous silent about it."

I looked at Blessing. "Do you trust me to?"

As an answer, her hand touched my face, her fingers wiping free what remained of a few raindrops. "Course I trust you."

"It's foolish to trust everybody," I said.

Blessing nodded. "S'pose so. Yet it'd be real empty a life to trust *nobody.*"

"Who's down there? Justice?"

"Probable so. It's his still."

"Can we watch? I never have seen people make whiskey, and I sure would like to learn how."

"Keep your voice down. It's real simple. I've helped Justice lots of times, and so's Hem. All you do is sour your corn mash until it's ripe as ready."

"How long does that take?"

"Days. Depends on the weather. When it's hot, the mash'll work up to a sour sooner. All it takes is corn and sugar and water."

"What's that copper thing over the hearth?"

"That's the cooker. And that long curly tube is called a worm. It condenses the corn vapor from the cooker, and cools it to liquor."

"How?"

"Justice says it works like a pitcher of icy lemonade on a hot day. Ever see a pitcher sweat on the outside?"

"Sure. Lots of times." I was surprised how much Blessing knew about cooking up corn whiskey.

"The cool of the pitcher squeezes the water in the air and it sweats the pitcher. That's why it takes plenty of cool running water to freeze your worm."

Below us, hidden among the dripping trees, I counted three men moving about. Their shirts were off. Stilling looked like hot work. One of the men was thickset, his chest sprouted a cop of white hair that matched his beard. It was Justice Lion. The three men were not talking, but working silently, feeding hardwood into their furnace and tending the barrels. Hem was there, too, adding a fourth hand.

We crept closer.

The copper gleamed in the sudden afternoon sun, a welcome sight after a rain. One of the men had cut a young tree, about ten feet long, using it to fan away the smoke. I guess I knew why.

"What's that funny thing atop the cooker?"

"That's the cap."

"Oh."

"Don't you downhillers ever still whiskey?"

"No," I said. "Not very often."

"Justice calls it his art. He's right careful. Keeps the copper clean inside, and slushes out the barrels and worm after each run. He claims there's no better whiskey in all of Vermont than his'n."

"I bet so. What's he do with it all?"

"Trades it off. On account of up here, where they aren't any roads, it's a whole mite easier to cart a few jugs of whiskey than it be to wagon a load of corn. And it'll bring a like price."

"Makes sense."

"Justice don't like much government."

"Well, I reckon the government's not too happy with Uncle Justice about now."

"A man's got rights to still."

"That's what Father says."

"He does?"

"Yup. He says that if Congress made fewer laws, and men like your pa made more whiskey, we'd all have ourselves a happier life."

One of the men worked a long pole to stir a mixture that I could neither see nor smell. Removing his pole, he sloshed it clean in a tub of water. Then I heard the clinking of glass greeting glass.

"What's that stuff called?"

"Beer."

"Is it really *beer?*"

"Not drinking beer. They just call it beer when the corn mash is sour enough to run through. Beer is just ferment corn."

"I see."

Blessing's head leaned over close to mine, as we lay on our bellies, watching the work. "You plan on raising a still down in Liberty?" She pinched me to let me know she wasn't serious.

"Not me."

"Well, if'n you do, best you get Hemming or me to help you hide it good. Your *place* is the most important."

"How so?"

"Cold water's first. Got to be cold and constant running, and clean. Build your furnace in a thicket of quick-growth greenery, like sassafras. Or laurel. And to mask your still when you're not around, never cut branches."

"Why not?"

"Cut branches will wither and turn brown. Justice says to always bend growing saplings over the still, so the leaves stay freshy green."

"Fine. Then what?"

"A path. Don't ever make no path to your still. Justice says he always nears his still from a new direction. And when the mule's packing in sugar or corn, lead her to the furnace from the uphill side. That's another trick, how to buy sugar. Down in Liberty, storekeepers know that when a man trades for a fifty weight of bag sugar, that he just might be up to more than baking pies."

I laughed. "I'll remember that. How does Uncle Justice get his sugar?"

"Down in Liberty, after dark."

"Where?"

"A woman named Bly."

I couldn't breathe. Against the wet earth, my heart sounded beat upon beat, as though I was hearing news that was best left unheard.

"I don't believe it. Honest?"

"Truly do."

"Petunia Bly?"

Blessing gave a quick nod. "But she's not the only supplier. They's others. And all womenfolk, most that claim they buy up bag sugar for church suppers and socials. Stuff like that. And you best not ever tell, Muncie Bolt, not if'n you expect to ever court *me.*"

"I'm no tattle-teller."

"Of course you're not. That's why I trust you. And old Justice trusts your pa. He said as much. My pa even trusts Rake Tatum."

I said, "Mr. Tatum's got a tough job, being sheriff."

"Now, I didn't say that exactly right. Rake Tatum's a good man. He even comes to supper once in a while and takes a drink from the jug. But he never asks where it come from, and old Justice, he sure don't spout up the information as to where he hides his still."

"Reckon not."

"One time, old Justice even gave Rake Tatum a mason jar of white to take home for Christmas."

"What did Rake say to that?" I asked.

"He said thanks."

"I wonder how come Sheriff Tatum doesn't ever arrest your father. Hold on. I bet I already know the answer. Because earlier today I was talking with Mr. Tatum, and I asked him if he was catching any lawbreakers."

"What did he say?"

"He said . . . only the bad ones."

"Sheriff Tatum and old Justice neighbor pretty well, since probable before you and I got born."

"I think my father might agree to that. Even though he practices the law, Father sort of believes in folks being left alone to do as they dang please. As long as what they do don't hurt anybody, or burn down somebody's barn."

Blessing sighed. "That's why I hate so much government. All that laws do is meddle and stir up."

"Father admits the same. He claims that some laws hatch more misery than they cure."

"You like your pa a lot, don't you?"

"Yes'm, I sure do. Father's good company. We live alone, just the two of us, and I guess we manage better than most. Say, you can come to eat supper with us sometime. If you want to."

"I want to."

"You will?"

Blessing nodded. "I'd like to meet your pa and listen to him talk about the law."

"He's real proper at that."

"Muncie, when you get to working, out of school and all, are you going into the law business?"

I couldn't answer. No, I wanted to say, because I want to be a preacher. I want to read the Bible just the way Father read for the law. He never went to a law school. But after he'd read the law, he passed his bar examination and got the third highest mark in the entire State of Vermont; I got told that by Henry Gleason. However, I couldn't tell anyone, not even Blessing, that I wanted to be a minister, because my father wanted me for a law partner.

"I don't know. Leastwise, not yet. What do you want to be?"

"A mother."

Thinking about what almost happened back in the pines made me swallow. I was real glad that I didn't put a baby into Blessing Lion. Maybe someday, but not right now.

"Maybe I'll make whiskey," I said.

"Not down in Liberty you won't. Besides, it costs a dear dollar to build a still."

"It does?"

"Well, you have to buy all that copper. Justice says that's the main expense. When you move your still to a fresh hiding, the things you take are always your cooker and the worm."

"Sounds like a bother."

"Justice says that it's a business with drawbacks."

"Like which?"

"Well, he says that to commerce his moon is about as risky as cooking it."

"S'pose it is."

"And it's hot work. Pa's got burnt all over himself. Scorches on his skin most everywhere you look."

"I bet Rake Tatum took notice."

"Reckon he did."

"What did he say?"

"Nary a word. Him and Pa don't talk a whole bunch. Them two, they just sort of stand shoulder to shoulder and look at the sundown, like two souls in church."

I smiled. "That's what Father and I do sometimes, after supper."

"More folks ought to do likewise."

"But I can't stop wondering why Rake doesn't arrest your pa. It's his job."

"Justice knows that."

51

"You mean Justice buys him off?"

Blessing Lion gave my rump a slap. "No. Because old Justice wouldn't offer and Rake Tatum wouldn't take."

"Father says Mr. Tatum's honest."

"So does Justice."

"Then it sure is a mystery to me how your daddy keeps himself out of the jailhouse."

"Pa says it's due to quality."

"I don't understand."

Blessing sighed. "Justice claims that what he draws off his still is pure and unhurtful. But if'n he was to cut corners and run cheap, and cause some drinker to take sick, that's when Rake and his sow-pig would come snooping."

"His *pig?*"

Blessing nodded. "Her name's Deputy. Plenty of times I heard Justice and Rake laugh about it. And the tales he can tell."

I shook my head. "Well, I guess I knew Rake Tatum kept a pig out back, but I didn't know her name was Deputy."

"He trained her. Justice says that Sheriff Tatum don't slop that pig like regular."

"How does he do it?"

"Pa says he feeds her sour mash corn. Hides a pan of it back in the woods, so Deputy has to go sniff it out. He tucks it off real far so she'll work the woods like a hungry hound."

"Wow," I said. "Like a bloodhound smells out a human scent, and tracks."

Blessing winked. "Justice tells that Rake Tatum's got his sow so trained that she could put her snout to the earth and rut out a still at the North Pole."

"So that's the reason Sheriff Tatum doesn't keep a dog. Instead, he's got himself a sow that can smell out a still."

"Truly be."

"Yet he only uses Deputy to go after the folks that don't manufacture good whiskey."

"Quality," said Blessing. "He must reason that Justice is a quality man."

"Must be."

"And my pa thinks equal of Rake Tatum. So they come to a truce. That's what Justice says they have between."

"A real truce."

"Pa don't churn up grief for the law, and the lawman abides it."

"Is that how Uncle Justice puts it?"

"Muncie, it ain't to be talked about, hear? Not when you go back among the downhillers, in Liberty."

"Do you trust me, Blessing?"

"With all my heart and soul and body. Because if you was to even whisper what we talk on, to any ear, then I vow we'd not again kiss."

As she spoke, Blessing Lion's pretty face clouded to sober.

"That's not the reason," I told her.

"What is?"

"Your trusting me. Trust is grander than kissing. Liars can kiss. And drunks on Saturday night. People might even kiss while they hold a lie in their hearts."

"A promise is plenty sweet," said Blessing, "but what's more dear to me is the keeping."

Chapter 7 ❧

L et us bow our heads."

We joined hands in a circle. Closing my eyes, I let the fragrance of butter-boiled potato sneak up my nose. Along with Dolly Lion's rabbit pie. Yet I didn't even peek, waiting for Justice to clear his throat and rumble his thanks:

"Lord, we thank Thee for the bounty of our table, for our friends, our home. Cleanse our souls, dear Lord, and gut out what be foul. Just as Dolly done with them two rabbits. Amen."

"Amen," we echoed.

Dolly Lion was a wren of a woman, as small as Justice was big. I took notice of her face and how she smiled after every blessing. No doubt appeared in her eyes that a Lion grace went right up to where it was intended to be heard, and recorded, in some golden ledger.

"Muncie," she said, "it's good to supper you."

I was hoping that she wasn't going to comment on the fact that Hem was built thicker. She forked the largest potato onto my plate, where it steamed like a white coal. Uncle Justice nudged the pie in my direction. Beneath the tawny crust the cooked rabbit favored baked chicken.

"Help yourself, boy," Justice said.

"Dig in," said Dolly.

"Yes'm, I sure will."

"I'm fixin' to tell your pa," said Justice, "that you cotton to Dolly's meals better than to his'n."

"I like both a whole lot," I said.

"Stout lad."

"But what I really enjoy is when we all hold hands while you say the grace." What I pleasured in the most was holding the hand of his daughter.

Dolly said, "Fitting and proper."

"Gratefulness," said Justice, "be the highest verse of prayer."

"Amen," said his wife.

Across the table, on the other side of the rabbit pie that Hem Lion was spooning out onto his sister's plate, sat Blessing. The women of the Lion household were served first. With one exception, and that was for guests, like me.

"Thank your daddy," said Justice to me, "for that can of store-bought peaches that he made you fetch up to us, Friday last."

"Sure will. I already have."

Hem fired off a warning look in my direction. But he had no cause to worry himself over whether or not I was going to drop the crockery.

"Dang them thieves," muttered Justice. "Picked our peach tree near to empty and run tail off."

Most of the peaches had, a month back, disappeared down the gullets of Hemming Lion and Muncie Bolt. We'd near eaten a dozen apiece. So the can of peaches for Uncle Justice had been my idea, to pay back what we had helped our bellies to.

"If'n I catch that varmint . . ."

"Gentle," said Dolly.

"Yes'm."

Perhaps it was Uncle Justice who was the King of Kipp's Mountain and all its clan of Lions, yet at the supper table, Dolly was head hen. The shack where they lived was a two-story structure; the loft for sleeping, but below the ladder was one room, mostly kitchen and a table. And indoors, Dolly ruled her massive husband and growing children.

Blessing hadn't said a word.

Her eyes favored me a twinkle. Was she still remembering, as I was, her being birth naked with me in the rain? I sure recalled it.

"More pie, Muncie?" asked Dolly.

My plate had three more forkfuls, plus a half-eaten biscuit. But I nodded to another serving of rabbit which was too mouthwatering to pass up.

"Put some beef on your bones," Justice said.

I hated being called skinny, even though I was a long way off from fat. When, I wondered, would I ever muscle out into looking like Hem?

The cat came.

Earlier, prior to our sitting to supper, she had been curled up behind the big black cookstove. Over she strolled, to jump up into the ample lap of Justice Lion, and even from where I sat, I heard her purr. Justice had named her Dearly, according to what Blessing had reported. Her full name was Dearly Beloved Lion.

"Sweetkins," said Justice, "are you hungry?"

At the sound of the deep voice, Dearly's purring swelled louder. I saw Hem look at his mother. Dolly Lion seemed as though trying not to smile.

"The way," she chirped, "*some* folks baby a cat. Near to borders on shameful."

I saw her hand reach over to stroke Dearly Beloved's ear, and then pat Justice a turn or two on his chubby knee.

Hem ate like an army. I counted at least six biscuits, with honey and butter, that went his way, and stayed. He downed more than Justice and about as much as Blessing and I as a pair.

"Mama," he said, "I'm beholding."

"Save room, son."

Hem smiled a grin at me that near to exploded off his face. That, I knew, meant dessert. I wondered what it was. A week back, Dolly had made what she called a peach cobble, using the cangoods I'd presented, in guilt.

"I sure love peaches," I said.

Pain stabbed my shin just ahead of the toe of Hem's boot. Whether he'd heard the crack or not, Justice looked up from whispering baby talk to Dearly. My leg hurt so much that it popped open my mouth.

Justice smiled. "It'd be a sorry sunup when I'd refuse peaches to Jesse Bolt's lamb."

He knows?

That was when Hem laughed. "Lamb," he sort of giggled my way. "Blessing had a little lamb . . ."

His sister's fist caught him in the ribs and it sure smarted enough to sober his mirth. But he didn't punch her back.

"Enough," said Dolly. "Unless the pair of you are fixing to turn away from what's in the warming oven."

"Lambs," said Justice, "ever frolic. And that's their beauty."

"Not at a table."

"Yes'm," said Hem.

"He starts it," said Blessing.

"A shame," said Dolly Lion, "that what's in the oven'll fetch out back to the hogs."

"I'm sorry, Mama," said Hem. "Both us."

"Best you be."

"Funny thing about my peaches," said Justice. "I been blaming old Dearly here, on account they vanished so sudden. And just about the same day I was fixing to harvest. For the woman to put by."

Dolly said, "Ain't that a caution."

"I don't suppose," said Justice, "you two boys would know where all my peaches melted off to."

Hem kept quiet.

"One," said Justice. "Whoever it was, the rascal left me *one* little old peach."

"And that 'un," said Dolly, "he brung to me."

"Reason be," said Justice, "is because you know the gal I do truly worship. It be Dearly." His big laugh infected us.

The four of them (five, counting the cat in Justice's lap) shared a family feeling that I envied. Even with my eyes open I could still read the note that I'd left on the kitchen table at home, telling

Father that I was going uphill and wouldn't be back for supper if I was still missing by six o'clock.

I thought about my father, eating alone, because I wanted to be with the Lions. The picture in my mind made me want to jump up from the table and run home. And to hug Father, just to tell him that he and I were still a family. The pang in my gut turned me a mite sour, and I wasn't so sure about wanting any of Mrs. Lion's dessert. Even if it was, by some miracle, another peach cobble.

My plate was finally empty and I was full. I wanted to look at Blessing, the way I did in school, but was afraid to have Uncle Justice catch me. I don't guess he, or her ma, knew about Blessing and me. He probably just figured that I wandered uproad to visit Hem who was my pal. Well, I'd just let old Justice think his pleasure, while I'd continue to dwell on my own.

Blessing cleared the table, while Dolly opened up the warming oven. What she withdrew opened up our eyes.

"Shortcake," she announced. "With some strawberries and cream, if the cow's still sweet."

The strawberries weren't the big kind that sold in the grocery store down in Liberty. Instead, they were the wild variety, no larger than glassie marbles that a kid could flick one through a circle in the dust, I was thinking.

Hem ate his shortcake in nearly one bite, as a riverlet of cream ran down his chin. It looked as though Hem might have welcomed a shave. Darn it. My own jaw didn't sport even one solitary whisker.

"Boy," said Hem, "that shortcake, Mama, is a song."

Hem was right. Dolly Lion's strawberry shortcake tasted so good it made me almost hurt all over.

Justice drank hot tea from a cracked cup that was missing a handle. Only two broken-off stubs remained. With each steamy sip, his lips made a slurpy noise, causing Dolly to shoot him a look of warning.

"Manners," she said.

"Yes'm."

Hem and Blessing washed up the dishes in a bucket of hot soapy water, while Justice and Dolly and Dearly Beloved and I rested our meal at the table.

"Tell me, lad," said Justice, "what your daddy is doing these days down yonder in Liberty."

"Practicing the law, sir."

"Evenings, too?"

"He doesn't busy himself a whole lot after supper. Used to play poker with Henry Gleason and a few other men."

"No longer?"

I shook my head. "I guess since Mother died he sort of lacks the luster to socialize."

Justice tightened his lips. "Shame."

"A good man," said Dolly, "your pa."

"Yes'm, he is. Thank you."

Justice said, "It be us Lions that's got *him* to thank, boy. Ever and always. Years back, Jesse Bolt done me a turn when nobody else would take a poke at the problem."

"You mean about your son, Drury."

Justice Lion nodded.

"Father told me about that."

"What'd he tell you?"

"Well, about the homicide case and all, and how he drew the jury, even though Mr. Gleason, the district attorney, was watching over his shoulder."

"Wheelright was a cheat," said Justice. "Cheated my cousin and sold him a sickly mule. Colic."

"What's the colic? I don't guess I rightly know what it is."

"To you and me, boy, colic's no more than a belly ache. Gas in the gut. But it's grave serious to a mule or a horse."

"How so?"

"I seen a colic mule groan out a spasm that'd cry your heart to listen. Then she lay down and kicked to beat Old Harry. Kicked herself so hard that she knotted up her intestine, the large one, and begged for the shotgun to put her to rest."

"And my father knew this?"

"He done did after I told him. So maybe that's the reason he agreed, years back, to defend my Drury against the law."

The way that Justice Lion said *law,* I could tell that he wasn't too fond of it.

"I seen my boy, down in Liberty, before the days of that trial. And during. I seen him in a cage, like a trapped animal, his hands around them iron bars that prisoned him in that wee cell. I read the terror in his face."

"Because he might hang."

"No. Nary 'cause of the rope. Drury weren't no coward. Wasn't his bowels that was afraid. It was his reason. I told 'em that there was no cause to pen up Drury in the jailhouse, on account of when his trial come up, I give my word that I'd march him down into Liberty to face up."

"But they wouldn't agree, I bet."

Justice Lion shook his head. "No, they wouldn't hold for it. No bail. And I'd a raised up the money for it someways, or died trying. Ain't human. It ain't Christian to cage a man. And worse, to let the downhill folks pass through the jailhouse to stare at my boy behind his iron. Like he was some freak in a circus."

Dolly shook her head. "A sin."

"Every day," said Justice, "I come to the village and look into his eyes, and if an eyeball could scream, 'twas his. I was witness to the madness that was growing on his face. Growed like a tumor. Like his eyes was two goiters. And, the Lord Holy be my judge on this, it weren't the rope he was fearing."

"What was it?"

"Life in prison. There was talk in the town, on just about every tongue, that they'd not hang my Drury. That they'd be merciful and give him a life sentence."

"But they didn't."

"At the time, boy, we didn't know the outcome. So I prayed. I confess I begged on my knees to my Giver God that if Drury got marked guilty . . . he'd *hang*."

I couldn't say anything. All I did was stare at the granite face of Justice Lion, a man whose son had once been indicted for a murder.

"Drury was a wild tad. Sixteen, at the time. Unbroke as a meadow colt. Curly hair. Why, when he'd go for a swim in the swamp pond, his hair would dry into a crown of ringlets. Sort of like mine. Folks said Drury favored me more'n a mite, and that we sure didn't find him on our doorstep."

"People say I resemble Father."

Leaning forward, Justice squinted at my face, nodding his agreement. It pleased me.

"Anyhow, what I say is this. You can't pasture a kicker of a colt in no closet. It'll twist his mind."

"But your son got off."

"His body did, yes. But soon after that trial, Drury run off. Had to, on account he was spawned to live in the open, where he can look a sky and feel the rain wash his face. That jail down in Liberty illed his brain. I know it. Drury was wild, I admit, but never was he moonstruck."

"Is he still alive?"

Justice nodded. "Living up north, near the Derby Line nigh to Canada. Yet he's only half alive. His sense is bent. They broke him in their dang jailhouse. I saw his face every day, every day."

"What did he look like, Uncle Justice?"

"Agony. Like a mule in colic."

Chapter 8 ✑

D ead?"
   As he looked at my father, Rake Tatum bobbed his hat just once. "The phone call come in while you were out of town, Jess. Thought you'd want to know about it, seeing as the two of you were associates."

The sheriff rested one foot on the bottom step of our front porch, switching his cane over to his other hand.

"Thank you, Rake. I'm appreciative that you walked over to tell me. I can't believe it."

"Heart attack, so they said."

"Well, he was getting on. Nigh to seventy. Hard to believe Horace Rudder's gone."

Sheriff Tatum spat. "He served that bench for near to a generation. We always got along."

"A good judge, Horace was. He'd pin back *my* ears more than once, if I ever acted too uppity in his courtroom. Never smiled. Folks said that if Judge Rudder ever grinned he'd rip his trousers."

Father and I stood on the top step of our veranda, looking down at Mr. Tatum, listening to the bugs of evening sing their August song.

"Set a while, Rake."

"Nope, can't stay. Miss Penny's home to her lonesome, and she fidgets some after dark unless I'm with her."

"Your sister's a fine lady, Rake."

"That she be. Penny's all I got in the world, so best I don't bungle the job. Even though it's a blame wonder she ain't died off on my cooking."

"Well, you're more than welcome to sit, Rake, if you can spare the time."

Sheriff Tatum did not answer. Removing his haymaker, he wiped the gray fuzz over his ears, using a blue bandana that he then re-folded to his pocket.

"Darn," he said, "I near to forgot."

"More news?"

"Yup. It's about Henry Gleason. He's got appointed as the new county judge."

Father pursed his lips. "If anyone deserves it, it's Henry. He's always been a dedicated D.A."

"That he has."

"*Judge* Gleason," sighed Father. "I must confess, that's a fitting title, even though it may be awkward for me to pronounce it."

"From what little I know of the law," said Rake, "I've observed over the years that Henry Gleason always does his homework."

Father agreed. "He certain does. And I ought to know, on account that I've gone up against him in court enough times. Henry and I don't always see things eye to eye. Yet he's a tolerable good lawyer. Best in town."

Nodding to me, Rake Tatum started to leave, but then turned to tap his cane on the slate of our front walk.

"You know, Jess, I was in that courtroom, years back, during the Drury Lion trial."

"So I recall."

"I saw you beat Henry Gleason."

Father chuckled. "That once was delicious, Rake. Absolutely delicious. And if you remember, it was Horace Rudder who honored the bench."

"So I recollect."

My father rubbed his palms together, as if he was still savoring his victory. "You know, it isn't every decade that a lawyer like me gets the upper hand on Henry. And he's never forgotten it. Says he doesn't recall too much about that case, yet I know he could recite every line of testimony word for word, along with Horace Rudder's charge to the jury. In fact, I'd bet a new bonnet that Gleason could tell you the precise number of times that Judge Rudder used the term *beyond a reasonable doubt.*"

"Quite possible. But if I be you, Jesse, I'd conclude right sudden that you'd best not tease Henry about it. Now that he'll be swore in as Judge Gleason."

Father, dressed in his shirtsleeves, hooked his thumbs beneath his purple suspenders. "Guess who, Rake?"

"That's easy. We all seed Henry Gleason take a stance like that in the courtroom. Thumbs up, as if he was about to inform the jury the big news that they'd discovered salt in the ocean."

Thumbs still hooked, Father began to drum his fingers on his shirt front, which I recognized as his own impersonation of Mr. Gleason. My father played the part well; and if Rake Tatum was the kind of man who grinned, I think he'd almost cracked one open.

"Dang you, Harry!"

All three of our heads turned in the direction of the Bly household.

"Must be a full moon," Father said. "That's usually the time that Petunia Bly and her husband have at it, and throw a frying pan or two. Guess you'll have to pay 'em a call, Rake, just to preserve and protect poor Harry from bodily harm."

"Nope, not me. My salary ain't so fat as to risk a tangle with Petunia when she's got her Irish up."

"For sure," said my father.

"I'd stay healthier if I was to pick a scrap with Justice Lion. Guess I'd rather stand toe to toe with *three* of him, compared to one of Petunia."

Father and I watched Sheriff Tatum limp down the front walk, through the gate, and toward home. I could still hear the scraping of his shoe even after he was out of sight in the dark.

"Rake's a solid soul," said Father.

"Do you like him?"

"He's a good law officer, Muncie. Even though he looks the other way, at times. Sort of a judge and jury in his own right, which, as a member of the bar, I cannot publicly approve."

"I guess Miss Penny's still ailing."

"Always will be. Rake Tatum's never grabbed much living for himself. Just seems content to live with his sister and tend to her. He's been brother, nursemaid, and cook for that lady ever since I can remember. Maybe that's why Rake never got wed. Never moved out into marriage, or worse, brought home a bride. Two women under one roof would have proved less than tranquil seeing that one's a hopeless invalid."

"I heard that Miss Penny can't walk."

"Correct. Skinny as he is, Rake helps lift her up, almost carries her around. Luckily she's frail enough to constitute a light burden."

"He's a real brother."

"That he is, son. And his sister is what makes life worth living for Rake. Years ago, Miss Penny fell off a mare and never walked since. Damaged her spine, at least that's what Doc Goodall told me. Rake was riding the horse at the same time. Bareback. Banged up his leg."

"Must be pesky."

"Rake's had a passel of medical bills to foot. Yet I don't guess I ever heard one word of complaint from the man. Literally and figuratively, our sheriff bears his burden. In silence."

"I'm glad I'm not a burden to you."

"*You?* Why you couldn't be a burden if you tried all night."

I smiled at him. "Thanks."

"The other evening, when you and Hem went cooning, I imagine you tried darn near *half* a night to turn yourself into a tribulation."

"Reckon so."

"But you survived. A boy your age has to go rambling after sunset. I don't suspect I'd have me much of a bullcalf if I was to pen you up, like a pig in a sty."

"Rake Tatum keeps a pig."

"So do most folks. What's so uncommon about raising your own porkchops?"

"She's a sow. Her name's Deputy."

Father laughed. "Hah! Yes, I do remember now, as someone told me that as a fact. Sounds like a fitting name for a sheriff's pig."

"But I heard that Deputy's not getting raised as bacon. She's sort of something else."

"Like what, son?"

"Deputy's his bloodhound."

Father stopped rocking, holding the armrests of his chair very still, looking at me. "Muncie, I'm not going to fib with you, or try in any manner of speaking to jerk you around, from one philosophy to another."

"I don't understand."

"Precious good. Because I don't either. All I can say to you is a phrase that people in town, and out of town, repeat."

"Which one?"

"*It's the times.* What they mean is Prohibition, but no one seems to want to say it. Instead, they say . . . it's the times. As though we are now groping through some dark age of the human condition."

"What kind of an age?"

"Possibly an era of mistrust. Muncie, I can't honestly say that I'm partial to whiskey."

"You don't drink at all."

"Hardly ever. But the point I'm so laboriously attempting to make, in my lawyerlike lilt and lingo, is this. I'm less opposed to drink than I am to people who order me to abstain."

"What's abstain mean?"

"It means to go without, to refuse to partake of something, usually meant to be for one's own bettering."

"Oh."

Father sat in one of the porch rockers. "Here in Vermont, way back in the year 1853, we enacted a statutory prohibition, which was subsequently supplanted by local option. A town can vote to go wet or dry. In a study of Vermont as a whole, the fact is that dry sentiments predominate. Yet in those jurisdictions, there was little or no law enforcement. People did as they damn well pleased. And still do."

"Is this how Rake feels?"

"That would be my estimate, yes. Constables and sheriffs in Vermont get elected by not harming the unharmful. Oh, a spank here and there. A wee fee, or fine, and a night or two as guests of the jailhouse. Little more."

"I see."

"Then along came October of 1919, only four years ago, when Congress in Washington passed the Volstead Act."

"What was that?"

"Prohibition . . . our great and noble effort to change humanity."

"I guess it didn't change Mr. Bly."

My father tossed back his head and I enjoyed hearing his laughter. "No, my dear boy, it did not change the socializing habits of Harry Bly. Nor did it better Petunia's life even one whisker. I doubt she demands much federal assistance in correcting her husband."

"Is that funny?"

"Perhaps not so slap-knee jovial as I interpret. What I so revel in was your honest and chidlike simplification of a human situation, as a prototype, that should be equally obvious to those featherheads in Washington."

"I don't get it."

"Oh, *yes* you do. But my point is, *they* don't. Not down in Washington. Prohibition did not vary our dear neighbor, Mr. Bly, even one degree from his charted course atop a very *wet* sea."

"I got it."

"Of course. And what I find so refreshingly droll, yet so pathetic, is the fact that Harry Bly has ignored Volstead in the exact manner that Volstead originally ignored the character of Harry Bly."

"It's good to see you laugh."

"And it feels sublime. I shall worry about his honor, Judge Gleason, on the morrow. But not tonight. No indeedy, not when I have you to sport with and the government to chide."

"Father . . ."

"Yes?"

"We got to laughing about all this stuff because I was telling you about Mr. Tatum's pet pig."

"Quite. I digress, and a good lawyer doesn't do that, not if the bench is on its toes. Or on his. Remember that, when you hang out your . . ."

"You stopped."

Father shook his head. "Not in time."

"Just as you were about to say when I hang out my shingle and practice the law."

"Guilty. Guilty as charged. Very well, Muncie, I shall confess to you forthrightly. It is my most fervent hope that you will someday soon consider pursuing the law."

"It would mean a lot to you, wouldn't it."

My father's thin hand gently caressed the air before his face as if touching a new shingle.

"Bolt and Bolt."

"Which one can I be? The first or second?"

"We'll be a partnership, Muncie. And let the whole town guess as to which one of us is up front."

I couldn't tell him. Not now, not when he was so enthusiastic about my becoming an attorney, and being his law partner.

But I want to be a minister. Not a lawyer. I want to preach sermons and marry people and bury them, too. And baptize babies. It's the Bible I want to study, and not some dry old law book. I can't help it, Father, but that's the way I'm leaning. Yet I can't tell you about it. Not until I'm sure myself.

Those were the words that were hollering inside me.

"There's a new fellow in town. Arrived today. I shook his hand over at the courthouse."

"Who is it?" I asked.

"His name is Sternlock."

"Is he a lawyer?"

"No, at least I don't believe that he is. To be precise, however, I dare say that Mr. Sternlock is quite interested in the law and the manner in which law in Vermont is currently enforced."

"Then he's a cop."

"Sort of. Mr. Elmer Sternlock is a federal officer. An investigator, attached to the Bureau of Prohibition. I believe that bureau to be an arm of the U. S. Treasury Department in Washington."

"Is that where he lives?"

"Not at the moment. He's taken a room over at Mrs. Mather's boarding house."

"Tell me what he's like."

"A big man. As barrelchested as Reverend Dennison. Big hands. Shoulders that seem to pop right through his coat. A pot belly. You asked me if Mr. Sternlock was a cop. Funny, but when I first set eyes on the man, *cop* was the word that came crashing into my brain. He smokes cigars, rather furiously in fact, as though he wants to smoke an animal out of its hole."

I repeated the man's name. "Elmer Sternlock."

"There's an aura about him. Not quite an odor, as that would be too unkind a term to employ . . . yet it could not be called a fragrance."

"Not like perfume."

"Hardly. Our friend Sternlock reminds me more of a police *dog* than a police *man*."

"Like he's after somebody."

"Indeed."

"I bet it's got to do with Prohibition."

Father nodded.

"Who's he after?"

"According to our most recent 1920 census, we have about three hundred and fifty thousand folks here in Vermont."

"He can't be after all of us."

"No. My guess is that, as of the moment, our new Mr. Sternlock isn't after anyone in particular."

"Good."

Beneath his chin, my father gently touched the tips of ten fingers together. "However, I do so earnestly believe that *one* of us will be caught."

"Who?"

"Son, I don't know. In fact, I seriously doubt that Elmer Sternlock knows. Or cares. Yet he's here in Liberty for a reason. A dangfool *government* reason, which, to my mind, constitutes precious little reason at all."

"Whenever you say *government,* it sort of sounds like you're underlining the word . . . or maybe spelling it out in capital letters."

"Hmm. Do I?"

"You sure as heck do."

"Muncie, I've oft thought that all government, or rather any hypothetical governing body, be it a monarch or a magistrate, is intrinsically the citizen's enemy."

"How so?"

"Anytime that you are awakened in the night and informed that the emperor's horse-soldiers have come for you, to escort you somewhere . . . this, my boy, is never good news."

"It's bad news."

"Truly so. To my way of thinking, perhaps the best government is the least government. Yet I fear that the authority in Washington swells each day. Like a gluttony."

"Thank goodness," I said, "that Vermont is a considerable ways away from Washington."

Father looked at me.

"Until today."

Chapter 9 🦢

I couldn't sleep.

Something kept waking me up. Blessing Lion was in my dream, here and there, and so was Hem and Uncle Justice. We all seemed to be eating, and playing baseball at the same time, which happens only in a dream.

Opening my eyes, I stared at the ceiling in my room. Then I heard voices, coming from downstairs in Father's office. One voice was deep and heavy, almost like the snort of a Holstein bull, but I couldn't quite hear any words. Only a low mumble.

I got out of bed, on tiptoe.

In our guest bedroom, the one next to mine, I knew about a cold air vent that was always open all summer, for ventilation. Looking down through it, I could see that a lamp was on in the study. Father was talking to somebody.

The man with the deep voice rattled off the names of several Vermont cities. "Burlington, Saint Albans, Montpelier, Rutland . . . these are the trouble spots, as we understand it."

My father replied, "I see."

"Now, I suppose you're wondering, Mr. Bolt, just what specifically brings me to your little town of Liberty."

"It has crossed my mind, Mr. Sternlock."

"Past experience has taught me a few tricks. In a city, there are too many people. I can't observe anything, or anyone, in depth."

"And here in Liberty you can."

"Yes. Looking at a map of Vermont, I concluded that Liberty could be the hub of activities which my associates and I have been authorized to remedy."

Father chuckled. "Liberty's a quiet town, Mr. Sternlock. I'm afraid you'll die of sheer boredom before you can even spot your first case of illegal parking."

"Is that so?"

"Fact is, motorcars aren't very plentiful in these parts. A new Ford costs a pretty penny, so most folks still drive horses."

"So I noticed."

"And lots still use oxen."

"What's your point, Mr. Bolt?"

"This isn't Chicago. I would imagine, based on what little gossip I've heard about bootlegging illicit whiskey, that such a profession would demand a faster pace than we slowpokes here in Liberty could whip up."

"Hah! And I presume that is exactly what you'd have me believe."

Both men were still for a moment. Holding my breath, I didn't even budge a muscle, waiting for the conversation to continue.

"I've already had a chat, earlier today, with Judge Gleason, newly appointed to the bench, I hear. And I plan on talking to every attorney and peace officer in the county."

"Mr. Sternlock, I'm sure we shall all be happy to cooperate with you as best we may. Also, I would conclude that Sheriff Tatum will be more than helpful with any records of known criminals."

"Excuse me for being a bit blunt, sir, but I'm getting the same answers from every soul in Vermont. Everyone's cooperative as all Hell, yet nobody *knows* anything."

"We're all simpletons?"

"Pardon me, but that's not at all what I meant. To put it another way, everyone I question talks a blue streak. Never before have I collected such a pile of worthless information."

"Well, I guess that negates the rumor, eh?"

"Which rumor?"

"The one that maintains how tight-lipped we Vermonters really are."

"Ah, but the rumor's true. You all are friendly enough, but no one *says* anything."

"Silence is golden."

"In criminal matters, Mr. Bolt, you know as well as I that silence is a felony. It's called withholding information, making any individual involved, an accessory."

"Ignorance is not a crime. Or has our federal government changed all that?"

"You're well aware that I have not come to Liberty to flush out *liars.*"

Father's chair creaked as he shifted position, draping a foot on his knee. "No, I suppose not."

Up through the air vent, I heard the rustle of a piece of paper being unfolded. Looking down, I saw Mr. Sternlock's hand pass the white paper to my father.

"Mr. Bolt, here are some figures that will substantiate our bureau's interest in your vicinity. Sugar sales."

"Don't tell me that you're planning an enterprise in the grocery business."

"Hardly. Your fellow citizens of Liberty consume about twice as much sugar per capita as they did ten years ago. The figures you're looking at represent, in hundreds of pounds, bags of bulk sugar delivered to Liberty by Green Mountain Wholesalers."

"Interesting. Yet, as I personally know so little about the grocery business, Mr. Sternlock, I can't draw much of a conclusion."

Sternlock snorted. "Well, I can."

"And how do you conclude?"

"Mr. Bolt, if all of you honest people in Liberty were consuming this much sugar, you'd all weigh over two hundred."

"Lots of our local ladies bake cookies for the church socials. And throw parties and the like. A tea now and again. Since the war, I reckon the town's a whole lot more festive, compared to five years ago."

"I can't swallow that."

"Besides, our town's growing. Sugar consumption is bound to rise. . . ."

"Per capita, Mr. Bolt. What the bureau wants to find out is this. Who's buying all that extra sugar and what are they using it for? As if I didn't know."

"Cookies?"

"As you are a local attorney, sir, please allow me to remind you most respectfully, that you serve also in the capacity as an officer of the court."

"Indeed."

"So what's going on in this town of yours? Other than, as you say, a big surge in cookie baking?"

"Mr. Sternlock, it's hardly fair of you to assume criminal activity merely on the basis of a town's having a sweet tooth."

With his lean fingers, Father gently refolded the white paper, handing it back to his visitor.

"Sir, we know what's happening in this town of yours. All over Addison County. These are not just idle suspicions. There are other yardsticks. Traffic indications. This doggone county of yours is one big still."

"Those are strong words, Mr. Sternlock."

I saw a big fist pound a beefy knee. "You're darn right they are."

"Now if the bootleg traffic here is all you claim it to be, wouldn't the state troopers have nabbed a few of the offenders?"

"Sir, I also know how many state policemen Vermont can brag about."

"How many?" asked my father.

"Exactly nineteen. And even if they all worked seven days a week, which they don't, this means that on a three-shift day, all you have in uniform at any one given hour . . . in the entire *state* . . . is six."

74 ∂◑

"If that."

"You're so right, Mr. Bolt. Considering illness, vacations, days off, my guess is that about *four* motorcycle cops are on duty at this very moment. Four, in all of Vermont."

"Like I say, Mr. Sternlock, crime in Vermont never has been much of a problem. We're a peaceable people."

"Peaceable? Well, perhaps so. Nonetheless, all indications point to a current rash of criminal activity . . . moonshining . . . in this area. It cannot continue."

"How do you aim to stop it?"

"We have ways, Mr. Bolt. Your federal government is a rather large and far-reaching organization, and we fully intend . . ."

"Excuse me, but you suddenly spoke as if *you* yourself are the the government, acting against *us,* the people."

"Well, I suppose I do represent the fed in this instance, yes."

"It was sort of my understanding that the government in Washington was supposed to be *all* the people. Not just the men in your bureau."

"Of course, of course. Needless to say, the Volstead Act was passed by Congress, which proves it's the people's will."

"Does it?"

"Naturally. Look, I don't want to argue politics with anyone, Mr. Bolt. I'm here in town to represent law and order, and to assist local authorities in the apprehending of felons."

"Helping us crack down on crime."

"Exactly. I've had a brief talk with Sheriff Tatum, and between you and me, Mr. Bolt, there's a fellow who probably needs a lot more manpower than he himself realizes."

"Possibly."

"Does he have a deputy?"

Hand over my mouth, I fought producing an outright giggle that Father and Mr. Sternlock would overhear. I tried not to think about Rake Tatum's pig.

"Not to my knowledge."

"You see?"

"But he's never *needed* one. As I earlier stated, Liberty's a quiet little town."

"On the surface, perhaps. Nothing but hayfields, meadows, milk cows, and a battalion of cookie bakers."

"You make us sound so poetic."

"We're not being fooled, Mr. Bolt. We know. Rewards have been offered, and I can tell you that money produces informants."

"How comforting to learn where my federal taxes go, to inspire me to inform the authorities about my neighbor."

"It gets results."

"Yes." Father sighed. "I quite imagine so. Yet are the results that it gets the goals of our society?"

"Are you saying, Mr. Bolt, that all laws are not to be enforced?"

"Not quite. Perhaps what I'm saying is that all laws ought first to be periodically examined. Because, as I see it, inadvertently a certain law might be passed which in practice could prove to be a law that cannot equitably be enforced."

Sternlock grunted. "All laws can be enforced."

"Really?"

"Bank on it. Force is what people understand, and respect."

"And honor?"

"We're getting off the subject, sir. Legal philosophy and jurisprudence are not what I came to discuss with you."

"Why did you come?"

"I'm looking for a place to start. That's what the Attorney General said recently. You have to start with people."

"In order to induce them to betray one another."

"Yes. Well, *no* . . . not quite. The Attorney General has his office to fulfill."

"Don't we all. You know, Mr. Sternlock, if I were the President of the United States, can you guess whom I would appoint as the A.G.?"

"Who?"

"Seeing as I am a Republican, I would appoint the best doggone Democrat I could find."

"That's odd."

"Yes, it is. But that's what any President ought to do. Never appoint a crony, or an alter ego to the post. And, most of all, never appoint a relative."

"Why not?"

"Because, in my opinion, Mr. Sternlock, that would constitute a total lack of morality. It would be only a power grab. And the people, God love them, would be up in arms."

"Mr. Bolt, you're a refreshing man to chat with, but infuriating . . . the way you constantly lead me away from my subject."

"Oh, your subject is capturing Vermont citizens who currently behave in contrast to the Volstead Act."

"Exactly that. I don't pretend to be an expert on whether or not a certain law is just. I'm only an enforcer."

"I'll help you all I can."

"Here's where I plan to start. With foodstuffs."

"Ah, I shall be most interested in this."

"How many grocers do you have in Liberty?"

"Let's see . . . Turner's, Lundt's, and Showalter's. Those are the three. Sugar, I presume, is what you intend to keep tabs on."

"Correct. I want the name of everyone in town who comes into a grocery store to purchase sugar. And the amount they carry out."

"How about their fingerprints?"

"You're pulling my leg, Mr. Bolt."

"Am I? Thought for a moment that you were pulling mine. To use a term, perhaps you were yanking the shank of Liberty."

"No, I'm deadly serious."

"So I see."

"I'm not thoroughly convinced, Mr. Bolt, that we'll get the goods on these sugar buyers, but it'll make 'em wary. Maybe, in my own way, I can cut down on the whiskey manufacturing in this locale."

"I'm sure you can."

"What I'd like to know is, will the three grocers in your town be cooperative? Or will exchanges occur under the counter?"

"Tough question."

"You mean to admit that, in your experience, the grocers here are in cahoots with the moonshiners?"

Father cleared his throat. "Hold on. It would hardly be ethical for an attorney-at-law to pass comment on his neighbor's standards of behavior. Some of these folks are going to sit on a *jury* that I shall have to face."

"That shouldn't matter."

"Perhaps not to you, sir, as you're new in town. But I have to live here, raise a son, pay my taxes, and attempt to earn us a living stipend."

"I see your point."

"Wouldn't you have better luck if you postponed this sugar-watch of yours, and perhaps considered other areas of sleuthing?"

"Name some."

"Easy now, Mr. Sternlock. As you know, I am not a detective. I usually leave police work to professionals, like you, and Rake Tatum."

"You'd call *him* a professional?"

"Matter of fact, yes. Perhaps not by those lofty standards you set down in Washington, but for our contented little nest here in Liberty, I think Rake executes his job just fine. And so do our voters."

"I saw your jail."

"Did you? Enjoy the visit?"

"There wasn't one damn soul in it. Every cell was as empty as a tomb."

"Must have been a quiet summer."

"If you tell me once more what a quiet town Liberty is, it just might disturb my digestion."

"Let our jail be my witness."

"Mr. Bolt . . . your empty cells prove one thing to me. It means that your sheriff isn't doing his job."

"Whoa. You're way ahead of me, Mr. Sternlock."

"In what way?"

"Rake's job isn't to fill the jail."

"Then you tell me what his job is."

"As I see it, Rake's job is to keep the peace instead of the prisoners."

"And to turn a blind eye in every direction, ignoring all the illicit activity that's happening right under his very nose."

Father laughed lightly. "Rake Tatum's nose is a bit longer, and more curious, than a good many folks imagine. Sometimes a friendly warning is enough to discourage some of our young hellions from getting themselves into trouble."

"I see. Then, as you see it, everyone in this quiet little town of yours is home this evening, baking cookies."

"Which reminds me," Father said. "Mrs. Bly, our next door neighbor, sent some cookies over just yesterday. Let me fetch you one, and brew you another cup of tea, if you're not in a hurry."

"What time is it? Must be close to midnight."

"Seven after."

"Gosh, I'll never get up."

"You will at Emma Mather's. Breakfast, I heard, was at six o'clock. Either that or you don't eat until supper. I'm glad you popped in, Mr. Sternlock. Always interested in learning what the law is up to."

Looking up at me through the grating of the cold-air vent, Father threw me a wink.

Chapter 10 ❧

"More milk?"

Draining my glass, I set it down on the kitchen table, before answering my father's question.

"No thanks."

Father smiled. "You're wearing a white mustache."

With a napkin I wiped my mouth. "There. Am I up to snuff?"

"First class."

"How come you're all dressed up in your black court suit? You look like you're expecting a retainer from a rich client who's delivering it in person."

"Wish that were true, son. No, nothing of the kind. But I am going to Horace Rudder's funeral."

"Where's it at?"

"Congregational church."

"What time will you be home?"

Father raised his eyebrows. "Now, as I see it, that is a question I should be asking my son, instead of the other way around."

"I didn't go anywhere last night."

"Only to the guest room."

"Guess I was curious."

"I believe, Muncie, that you owe me an apology."

"For overhearing?"

Father nodded.

"Sorry. I apologize. Gosh, I really wasn't trying to spy."

Father filled the kitchen sink with hot water into which he dumped our breakfast dishes. "How much of the conversation did you hear?"

"Not all of it."

"Good."

"I was sleeping and the talking woke me up, so I thought I'd listen in. I promise not to do it anymore."

"Thank you, Muncie."

I winked at him. "You're welcome."

"Generally speaking, dialogue 'twixt an attorney and his client is, by rights, confidential. Had our Mr. Sternlock been a client, I would have been embarrassed if he had suspected that someone was spying from above the ceiling."

"I understand."

"Fine. Don't repeat it, please."

"Is Elmer Sternlock looking for a lawyer?"

"Well, if he is, he failed to say so."

"He's looking for people who still their own whiskey, that's for sure."

Father rinsed a cup under the tap. "That he is."

I laughed. "Boy, you sure led that guy around the barn a few times."

"Did I?"

"Yup. When the two of you were talking about baking cookies, I darn near busted into a fit."

"That," said Father, "would have been a most unfortunate outburst, one which could have displeased both your dad as well as his visitor."

"I held back."

"Yet I sensed you were up there." He tossed me a dishtowel.

"Are ya sore?"

"No, but no more of it, Muncie. I have your word on that, which is binding enough for me. Elmer Sternlock was a guest in our home, and we both owe him the courtesy of seeing to it that what he discusses here is confidential. Agreed?"

"Agreed. Even though you and I might disagree with some of his methods."

"In a way, I'm glad that you overheard what we talked about. How much of it do you remember?"

"Not a whole lot. I was still half asleep, I guess."

"Just as well."

"How come you're glad I listened in?"

Father sighed, handing me a dripping coffee cup to dry with the dishtowel. "Well, because Mr. Sternlock has come to induce the citizens of Liberty to spy on each other, perhaps he deserves to be spied upon himself."

"Even if he's a cop?"

"*Especially* if he's a cop. People who are so blindly sure they are right, with the law on their side, can often act in the extreme."

"The law can't be on both sides."

Father looked at me. "Ah, but it can. And that, my dear Muncie, is the beauty of our legal system. There are *two* trays to be balanced, and weighed, on the scales of justice."

"I guess that's what a judge has to do in a trial. Look at both sides."

"Let's hope and pray he does."

Wiping a saucer, placing it on the proper pile on our cupboard shelf, I looked at him. "Hey, I bet I know what you're thinking."

"Name it."

I said, "I figure you're wondering what kind of a judge Henry Gleason will be."

"Hah! Very good, son. That was precisely my thought."

"And I bet you sort of dread your next trial, when Judge Gleason will be on the bench. Am I right?"

"Indeed you are. Although *dread* is possibly too strong a term."

Knowing that I could keep up with Father once in a blue moon made me feel happy. Sort of cocky. But I was still curious about what I had overheard.

"Is Mr. Sternlock going to stir up trouble?"

"Perhaps not nearly as much as he would enjoy. Yet, one worry nags me a mite. Elmer Sternlock just might stumble into a hornet's nest and get a passel of people stung. It could snowball."

"Snowball?"

"By that, son, I mean that his investigation here could have some serious repercussions. Folks here in Liberty might begin to be less than trusting. What he plans to do, from what I gather, is *buy* information."

"Money talks."

"Unfortunately, yes it does. You won't be the only spy, Muncie. Though I don't approve of your eavesdropping, at least you did it with no purpose of monetary gain. You are not planning to tell what you overheard to any authority, an action resulting in some-one's arrest or confinement . . . or to line your own pocket."

"Of course not." I wiped a fork.

"But you see, everyone isn't like you, son. Although I hate to admit it, there *are* individuals in town whose greed might over-power their loyalty to a friend or a neighbor. Or even to a relative."

"So you already smell trouble."

"Regrettably, I do."

"What's going to happen?"

"Maybe nothing. Elmer Sternlock could leave Liberty for greener pastures. Just pack his bag and light out."

"But you don't think so."

Father shook his head. "Hardly. He's here to uncover as many whiskey makers as he can dig up."

"Sort of the way Rake Tatum is."

"More than that, lad. Far more. Rake is the law, yes, but he's one of us. Born right here in Liberty. I don't know where our friend Elmer Sternlock was born, but I know he's been nursing on a government tit. There's a fanatic gleam in Sternlock's eye, as though he'd give a tooth to punish somebody, with a jail sentence."

"Wow."

"Ever since I can remember, I have always been wary of people who are obsessed with punishment."

"Thank gosh." I pretended to snap his behind with my towel.

Father smiled. "I know, I haven't laid a switch on you in at least ten years, which probably proves that I have been remiss in this obligation."

"Don't let it worry you."

"It doesn't. You're a rascal at times, and a bit shiftless, but I believe that you and I are honest with one another."

"We are."

"For example, I somehow realize that you do not yet manifest a yearning interest in the law. Or even a yawning interest."

I laughed. "Not a whole lot."

"Lawyers don't make up the entire universe. There are other professions that may tweak your curiosity. Science, medicine . . ."

I took a deep breath. "You know, someday I might want to become a minister."

Father looked at me. "You?"

"What's the matter? Don't you think I'm worthy?"

"Of course I do. I would be ever so proud of you if that's your decision. It's *your* life, Muncie. And if you decide to preach the Gospel, I'd sit in the front pew, and try like the Devil not to applaud every one of your sermons. Or throw confetti."

"That would be neat."

"Reverend Muncie Bolt. Hah! I must admit that this comes as quite a shock. How long have you been considering such a path?"

"A few years."

"A minister, my own son. I must confess that this will take me some time to get used to. You're serious?"

"Very."

"Congratulations. I'll be very proud of you, you know. My vest will pop a few buttons."

"You'd be prouder, I bet, if I was eager for the law, so we could be partners, and practice together."

"It's crossed my mind."

"I know. And if you want the straight of it, what bothered me the most was how I'd ever get around to telling you. But it sort of popped out."

"What made it?"

"Well, it was when you said things about punishment, and that you and I were honest with each other. Suddenly, I wanted to be as direct as I could, because you're one whale of a good dad."

"I appreciate that."

"You've been washing that same plate for about five minutes. It sure ought to be clean by now."

"Holy cow! My son in a pulpit."

"Not yet I'm not."

"You could change your mind. I did, when I was older than you are. Earlier, I had decided on medicine."

"What made you switch to law?"

"I saw old Doc Struder deliver a baby. But it was born dead."

"Gosh."

"That was enough for me. The experience made me decide that I'd leave the rigors of mortis and childbirth in the hands of the experts, like Doc and Petunia Bly."

"Mrs. Bly must be the expert of the whole world on having babies."

"A good woman, Petunia."

"You like just about every soul in town, don't you?"

"Some more than others. However, I would say you are correct, Muncie. Yes, the folks in Liberty are good people. A few narrow ones that can turn petty in matters of politics, or religion. Yet each one of us holds the right to nourish his own opinions."

"Even me."

"Naturally, even you. Though you're in your teens, you still have the right to express yourself on the issues. As you often do."

"After I heard some of the things that Mr. Sternlock was telling you last night, I got to thinking about them."

"Oh?"

"Far as I'm concerned, I think somebody ought to tell Justice Lion and his family that Mr. Sternlock's come to town. And the reason he's here."

Pulling the plug to drain the sink, Father dried his hands on the dishtowel, and looked at me. "Muncie, it would be my guess that Justice Lion already knows."

"How could he? Mr. Sternlock's only been in Liberty for a day or so."

"News travels fast in a small town, son. I'd wager that the Lions, even though they live away up on Kipp's Mountain, know a blessed lot that goes on in this village."

"What you're saying is that Uncle Justice has a few spies of his own."

Father nodded. "Justice Lion has friends aplenty around here. In the past, he's done a good turn to more than one soul in this county. And were he to ask a favor, even one that might defy the law, I would estimate there'd be at least a score of persons in this locale who would pay him his due."

"Like who?"

"Whoa. One thing I must make clear to you, Muncie, and that is the naming of *names*. I presume you notice the caution with which I often speak. In generalities, avoiding the specific."

"You do it all the time."

"Perhaps some people would label that a fault, being vague. But let me warn you about using a particular man's name, or a woman's, when you discuss any local concern. Do you understand why?"

"You don't want me to get anybody in trouble."

"Well, that's part of it."

"There's more?"

"I don't want *you* in trouble. Not with the law, or with people in town, and especially not with the Lions."

"You're not afraid of them, are you?"

"Up in the hills there are bears. At this moment in time, I do not fear a single one of them."

"So?"

"If I were up on Kipp's Mountain, confronting a bear, I might be more than just a bit apprehensive."

"I can understand that. Anybody would."

"What's more, son, if several black bears were to take a notion to come downroad and invade the streets of Liberty, all of them in a rage with fangs bared, I believe I would sprout my share of goose bumps."

Scratching my head, I said, "You're sort of comparing the Lions to a pack of angry bears, aren't you?"

"Am I?"

"You sure are."

"Well, so be it. There's sort of a truce, Muncie, between the town-folk and the hill people, if you know what I mean."

"I'm not sure."

"We sort of leave the Lions alone. We don't pester them and they don't bother us. But I wouldn't dream of climbing up there and poking around in certain activities that don't concern me. I advise you to do the same."

Fishing in his pocket, Father drew out his gold watch, to check the time. He snapped it shut again with a click.

"Are you late?"

"No. Besides, I rather enjoy these little chats that I have with you. I suppose it is every parent's duty to warn his child about certain pitfalls."

"But you've always encouraged me to pal around with Hem Lion. Leastwise, you never once told me not to go up there. Hem's a real friend, and I know that Uncle Justice likes you a whole lot, because he sometimes admits it."

"I like him, too."

"Well, I'm sort of confused."

"Alas, so am I. From what you tell me, Hemming Lion is going to turn out much like his old man. He's going to be another Justice Lion, and these are things that I welcome to hear about. A lot of Vermont is still a wilderness, and I'm grateful for that, because it would be a sad day when boys like you and Hem Lion no longer go coon hunting on a moonlit evening. Boys and dogs."

I scowled, wanting to tell Father that I wasn't too certain as to what he was driving at.

"Perhaps, my lad, I talk too much. Or worry too much. Thank

goodness there's a lot of your mother in you. You'll have balance, and judgment. More than that, I'm sure you are the kind of boy who wants to do right by people. And that's what life is about. Living in harmony instead of in discord."

"I guess I understand. Sort of."

"That's why I enjoy my practice. The law exists primarily as a force to promote peace between a man and his neighbor. Peace, not punishment."

"Maybe I never looked at it that way."

"And I always have. Lately, at least. If there is any one nation on Earth that personifies human variety, it is these United States of America. We have infinite variety of color, race, and creed. That's beauty, Muncie. Beauty is little more than variety, as I see it. And so I thank the Almighty that people like the Lions possess the fortitude to be different, to *vary* in their style of life."

"So do I."

"I have to run. But all I want to say to you is one more thing. Justice Lion and Jesse Bolt, the two of us, are as different as night and day."

"You sure are."

"And yet, I truly believe that what Justice Lion holds dear to his heart is not too foreign from which I so fervently admire."

Chapter 11 &

"Feel a bite?"

"No," I told Hem. "I was just sort of nudging my bait around, so it won't sink down into the mud."

Hem Lion slapped a bug. "Ought to be fixing to get light soon."

"What time do you reckon it is?"

"Aw, who cares. But if'n I was to hazard a guess, I'd say about a half hour earlier than sunup."

Hem and I were out in his leaky old rowboat. And there was here about as much water inside it as there was in the pond it floated on. My feet were soaking wet but I didn't care a whole lot. Snake Pond was about the size of a football field. Not a cabin in sight, even though it would have been a pretty and quiet place to live. The shores around us were lined with stands of white birch. A loon hooted, its lonely cry echoing off into the stillness.

As the seat of the rowboat was getting hard, my fanny was going to sleep again, so I twisted into a fresh position.

Hem said, "Now's the time. Catfish usual take themselves a feed right before dawn."

I yawned. Hem and I had been sitting in his boat for over two hours, and the only bite I'd felt had come from the hungry bugs that were feeding on me. The back of my neck itched like all crazy.

"Are you sure there's catfish in this pond?"

Hem said, "Sure."

"How do you know?"

"Well, on account my cousin Ernest hooked a ten-pounder last week, that's how."

"Boy, I'd sure like to do that."

Hem sighed. "We won't catch poop unless you shut up your mouth and keep mum. Every dang catfish in Vermont knows you're around and about."

"Fish can't hear."

"The heck they can't. Justice says a smart old catfish can hear paint drying."

"Okay," I said, "we'll just whisper."

"Maybe I was wrong," said Hem.

"About what?"

Hem snorted. "About trying to turn you into either a hunter or a fisherman. Looks to me like you don't take to any of it a whole lot."

"Sure I do."

The two of us were quiet for awhile, and I just sat on the hard boatseat, listening to the croak of the frogs. The pond sure was becoming misty, giving me the feeling that our boat was floating way up in the sky, in the middle of a cloud.

"This place," I told Hem, "reminds me of Heaven."

"I suppose you been *there,* too."

"No, and I don't want to go right away either. Not for another sixty years or better."

"Good," said Hem. "Last year, when you and your pa made that trip to Burlington, it was all you could talk about. I got so fussed-up tired of hearing about Burlington, that I darn near stuffed a rag in your face, to shut you up."

"Well, it sure's a whole lot more exciting up in Burlington than it is in Liberty."

"Ain't never been to Burlington, or Rutland, and I don't expect to ever go."

"I bet you sort of plan to live up here on Kipp's Mountain all your life. And not go anywhere."

"Right."

"Don't you ever get curious?"

"Nope, not much. I'm a Lion, and us Lions stay to home and tend to our own turnips. If you ask me, the world would be a lot more peaceable if more folks would do likewise."

"Hem . . ."

"Now what?"

"I thought I felt a nibble."

"Haul up your worm and we'll look see."

Up came my line. Squinting in the fog, Hem and I examined my bait. The worm had turned white.

"It's dead."

"Don't matter, Munch. A catfish ain't so all-fired particular. They don't go to Burlington, and feed themselves fat in all them fancy eating places, like you."

"I'm not fat."

"Nope. You're still as skinny as a dryspell bean. Me, I'm near ready to beach the boat and head back to the shack for a belly full of Ma's breakfast."

"We haven't caught a fish yet."

"That's the way of it."

I was always a bit startled at the way Hem Lion accepted things. Like no fish. Whatever came his direction, he just took, as if Providence intended it.

"You hungry?"

"Yes," I said.

"I'm near to starved in. My old paunch is scraping along my backbone and it's fixing to rub raw."

"You, me, and these damn bugs are all hungry. Everybody except the catfish that you claimed would just about jump into the boat."

"Guess they don't aim to," said Hem. "But now it's starting to get light. Sun'll come up near sudden."

The sunshine would be welcome. I shivered, moving my body so Hem wouldn't take notice of how cold I was. Father had suggested that I wear a sweater, but I hadn't taken his advice.

"You cold, Munch?"

"Not me."

"I am. Chilly and stiff. Doggone seat is harder than winter rock. And my hoof's asleep."

"Just a few more minutes," I said. "Maybe there's an old catfish underneath our boat right now, begging for breakfast."

Hem sighed. "I'll say one thing for you."

"What's that?"

"You sure are a believer. If somebody said there was pie in the sky, you'd shin up a rainbow, with a fork in your hand."

Looking up, I saw the gray of morning beginning to speckle with gold. Treetops were turning a pale yellow and it made me feel a bit warmer to behold it. The stars were gone, and I couldn't see any moon. Only mist. I wondered if Blessing was still abed. The thought warmed me.

"Hem . . ."

"That's me."

"Do you believe there's a Heaven up there?"

"Not as much as I'm convinced there's an Earth down here. Why?"

"Just wondered."

"Tell you the truth, Muncie, I reckon I believe in what's alive more than what's dead. Death is what old folks think on, because they neighbor it more than we do. Further along the path, maybe. I want me a life to live and a lady to love."

"Is that all?"

"That, old pal, is one hellbender of a start."

"Who's your girl?"

Hem smiled. "Somebody. She's real dear. And I don't even know her last name. But she lives a long way from here. Ten miles north, up toward Homerton, and her Christian name is May. I'm going to marry her."

I almost dropped the pole. "You *are?*"

"Only saw her one time. At a fair. But she saw me. We didn't even say howdy. She's going to be my first wife."

"How many wives do you plan on?"

"Womenfolk die off, so Justice says. He knows. He's had wives.

Ma is his third. It grieves him more than he lets on. Pa's got a heart of music."

"Yes, I'd say he does."

"You and my sister . . ."

I swallowed, not being able to do much else, especially speak. My fingers tightened on the willow rod.

Hem said, "I took notice. The way Blessing gives you the calf eye, and you at her in the same fashion. Can't say I'm opposed to it. Do you righteous love her?"

"Yes, I do."

"That's proper. I don't want no downroader to coondog after my sister with his hands and not his heart. You hitch on?"

"I understand."

"You going to wed Blessing?"

"Well, to be perfectly honest about it, I don't ponder it a whole lot. I just think about Blessing."

"That's natural."

"I want to finish high school."

"So does my sister. Darn if I can figure out why. Blessing just might be the first Lion to earn a . . . what's that useless thing you get?"

"A diploma."

"Yeah . . . that. She'll maybe become the first Lion to go English."

"What's that mean?"

"It's what Pa always says about hill folks that abandon our plain way, and go modern. Live in town. Dress fancy. Take up with new notions and work for wages, bow their heads to some boss in a trading store, or become a sawyer at a pulp mill."

"And that's going English."

"Yup. But it ain't for me, Munch. I fix to keep uproad and scratch out best I can. And seed May. Watch her belly grow and hear the cry of our babes. I don't want no young of mine to slave-chain down in Liberty. My sons and daughters are to stand proud, fear the Almighty, and not bother nobody."

"Maybe that's best."

"And not suffer grief from one living downroad soul that comes up yonder to pester at us. God mercy folks that poke up trouble, because I won't pity a pound of 'em."

Hem's pole lashed the water, mean as a whip, a sharp crack of sound that cut into the fog and the morning. A scar across the silence.

"Are you mad, Hem?"

"Yes, kind of."

"What at?"

"Them newcomers. Justice, he knows. Feds, he calls 'em all. Been here before, years back, but not concerning the stills. Justice heard about the new law. Says it could puff up into a real reacher, that Prohibition."

"Maybe we shouldn't talk about it, Hem."

"Somebody ought to speak up. All you voting downhillers ought to stand forth and jaw your piece about that law. But you won't. So that's why I don't aim to breed my kids to go English. Not this boy. People got to take a stance and face up, because Justice claims that people are more holy than laws."

"Doesn't your father ever vote?"

"Not no more. Years back, on election day, Justice and his brothers all went down to Liberty, in a downpour rain. And some official told 'em they couldn't vote."

"Why not?"

"He said because they didn't register. Had some frill-fancy roll of voters, but no Lion's name was listed. Justice got turned away cold. And I don't guess he ever went to town again, after that. Not even when the church caught fire. For him, to stay uphill and not help fight them flames, alongside the rest of the ablebodied, was a grief to Justice. He ain't built that way, not to help and lend out. Pa wept. Just to stay uproad and look down at the burning, and not offer. Justice Lion wept."

"I like your dad."

"So do I, Munch. Oh, he's booted my sweet bum from Hell to

breakfast when I needed it, and he'd do it again tomorrow. But he's got my respect. I don't guess I say out like this very often."

"I'm glad you did, Hem."

"Just wanted you to know, that's all. You ain't too often like the rest of 'em, downhill. Your pa and you got sense, and a soul in your breast, a feel for another man's hurt, so Justice says."

Hem boated his pole. Working the oars, he headed in toward the marsh of the shoreline. A pair of mallard ducks swam out, to run along the water until their beating wings lifted them into flight.

"Swift," I said. I thought of Blessing and me.

"Late nested, maybe." Hem pointed the rowboat into a fresh heading, and I knew that he did it so he'd not disturb the duck nest.

Hem hid the boat, bending green saplings over it, so that the leaves would not turn brown and catch unworthy attention. It reminded me of how Blessing told me the way to hide a still.

"No stranger'll see it now," he said.

There was no path to the boat. No clearing around it, as hidden as the nest of the ducks that we never did see, or look for. Carrying our poles, Hem Lion and I headed uphill for his home, and hot food. But then he abruptly stopped.

"Soft," he said.

Moving ahead, and hardly breathing, we crept along a shelf of gray rock that overlooked a wide view of greenery, treetops below. We climbed higher. Hem had heard something, yet he didn't seem anxious to share his suspicions with me, nor did I press for an explaining. Hem Lion was a hard apple to squeeze juice from.

Hem pointed a long arm. "Horses."

Below us, through the trees, I saw two men. They were talking, yet I could hear none of their words; only two voices. Both men were on horseback. In front of them walked what appeared to be a dog. The animal was large and white. Narrowing my eyes, I noticed that it was not a dog at all, just as Hem said one word.

"Pig."

Instantly I recognized one of the men, the man with a cane hanging from his saddle.

"Hey," I whispered, "that's Rake Tatum."

Hem Lion nodded.

"Who's with him, Hem?'

"The other guy's a Fed. He's fresh in Liberty. Justice seen him up here a day ago, on that same horse, pointed him out to some of us, real silent. Our cousin told us his name is Sternlock."

"He came to see Father."

I winced. Why did I say that? If only, I was hoping, I could reach out my hand and grab my words, and stuff them back inside my stupid mouth.

Hem stared at me. His face wore a new expression, and suddenly he was no longer the Hem Lion that I knew so well; becoming, in one split instant, a man I did not know at all. His face was cold . . . yet the sweat sprouted on his brow. Breathing hard, he rolled up the sleeves of his faded blue shirt.

"You can tell your pa, for me and Justice and all us rest, that he's got some funny friends."

"He's not our friend. But you are."

"Tell him anyhow, lawyer boy."

"Don't call me that, Hem."

"It's true."

"Okay, so my old man's a lawyer. He works for a living and earns an honest dollar, and I don't aim to be ashamed of my father. He's a good guy."

"What side is he on?"

Side? I didn't know there were any sides. Not like a war. Looking at Hem's bare arms, I saw the scars. Burns. I'd seen the same kind of mark along the arms of his father, Justice Lion. I remembered what Blessing had told me, about the hot work around a whiskey still. One of the burns on Hem's arm was fresh, staring up at me like a scarlet danger flag, a screaming red.

"I can read you, Bolt."

Hem's words made me ill, weak, afraid of what he'd say next. Or do. I wanted to run away from Kipp's Mountain and the Lions, to be back home in Liberty.

"You got the shakes?" Hem asked.

"No."

"Looks to me."

"Well, I don't."

"You want to fetch yourself down yonder and help that pig sniff the ground for corn mash?"

"No."

"Maybe that's where you belong. Down there alongside that pig of Rake Tatum's. You and Sternlock and the law."

"Uncle Justice trusts me. He said so."

"Nobody's trusting nobody. No longer. We all heard about Sternlock."

"Father talked to him. But he doesn't like him. Not one bit."

"Best you go home. I got me things to do. First thing, I got to go find Pa, and damn sudden."

"Are we still friends?"

Hem didn't answer. The forest silently swallowed him, as though he were a part of it.

Chapter 12 ❧

"**H**ere he comes!"

It was Mrs. Bly's voice that I heard. She was standing in front of her house, pointing up the street. People rushed out of their homes, all of them craning their necks beyond where Petunia Bly was indicating.

"He's coming, Father," I said.

"I know. He told Rake Tatum that he'd come into town at noon today. And if Justice Lion gives his word, he'll be here sure as Judgment."

"Everybody's talking about it."

My father nodded, getting up from his porch rocker. "Yes, that's understandable. Rake stopped by last evening and explained the whole matter."

"Do you think Mr. Sternlock is going to do what he threatened to do?"

"Possibly. I think he'd like to see Rake lose his badge. Rake thinks so, too. Seems like Rake Tatum was uphill yesterday, when Sternlock and his boys smashed Justice Lion's still, and made the arrest. That was the time, according to what Rake told me, that Rake exercised his county authority, and told Justice that he'd best come into town tomorrow, meaning *today,* and turn himself in."

"I hate Sternlock," I said.

"Easy now, son. He's just doing his job."

"I can see Uncle Justice. And two men following along behind him."

"Your eyesight's better than mine. Who's with him? His brothers?"

"No. It isn't anyone I know. Just two guys in dark suits."

"Sternlock's men. Or so I presume. I'm surprised that Justice Lion doesn't knock their heads together."

People at the edge of the road were muttering, repeating the name of Justice Lion in whispers, as if they were almost afraid to say it straight out.

Father sighed. Hand over his eyes, he shielded his vision, looking up the street at three approaching men. "This so reminds me of years ago, when Justice said that his son Drury would turn himself in. And the next day, into town they marched, Drury and Justice, side by side. Everyone staring at them yet they looked at no one. Eyes straight ahead."

"Will they put Justice in jail?"

"Yes, they will."

"And there'll be a trial?"

Father nodded. "Henry Gleason telephoned me this morning, before you were awake. He told me that Sternlock and the Feds want to make a big thing out of this arrest. Not just a fine but a test case."

"A jail sentence?"

"If convicted, yes."

"Damn it."

"Rake is heartsick. I know how rotten he feels to have played a part in it. That sheriff's badge is all he has, besides Penny. *He's* all she has, and Rake knows it. Rake Tatum told me, in confidence, that he feels like ripping that star right off his own shirt."

"Maybe he will."

"No, I rather doubt it. We all threaten to do more than we get around to."

"Father . . ."

"Yes?"

"Will you defend Justice Lion?"

"If he asks me. He hasn't made such request, so your question, son, is premature."

"Do you hope he asks you?"

"Yes, I do."

"I want you to be his lawyer. Boy, do I ever hope for that."

"Why?"

"Because you'll win. You'll keep Uncle Justice out of jail and teach Mr. Elmer Sternlock not to mess with Vermonters."

"I appreciate your confidence, Muncie, and I thank you."

It was sort of like a band was playing in my ears, yet there wasn't any music. No drums and no trombones. Only the sound of Justice Lion's big shoes, kicking the dust of the road, marching into Liberty. On his head was a black hat, with a wide felt brim. He wore a dark and shabby suit, a white shirt, no necktie. As the shirt was partly open, we could see the gray hair on his upper chest, just above the "V" of his shirt buttons. Yet we saw no lack of dignity.

Justice Lion didn't look our way. I expected him to do so; maybe even to grin, and wave to my father, but he only looked straight ahead. Behind, about three or four paces, marched the two men I didn't know by name. Elmer Sternlock's men. I wanted to bend over and pick up a rock.

"Shame!"

Turning my head, I saw Mrs. Bly shake her pink and soapy fist at the two Federal men. Her mouth was tightened into a firm line. Coming our way, she entered our gate and walked up the walk to our porch.

"Jesse . . . do something."

It was the first time that I had ever heard Mrs. Bly call my father by his first name. She'd always called him Mr. Bolt, to his face.

"Good day, Petunia."

"Good? An evil day if you ask me. Arresting a man like Justice Lion. I say we ought to all band together and take matters into our own hands."

Father patted her arm. "Easy."

"I'm so mad I could spit hornets. So's Harry. And so ought to be every decent Christian in this town."

"I know. Come up in the shade and cool yourself off."

"Hah! Fat chance of that. I'm boiling, Jesse. So heated up over this mess I can hardly breathe."

"Settle down, now. You'll live longer. Nothing very serious is going to happen to our friend Mr. Lion."

"Howdy, Mrs. Bly," I said.

For some reason, Mrs. Bly put her meaty arms around me, giving me a hug that stopped breath. "Bless your heart, Muncie. That's your pal's daddy out there."

"Yes," I answered, wondering if Hem Lion would ever again be my best pal. Asking myself if Blessing . . .

"Jesse, what'll we do?"

"Nothing right now."

"Nothing?"

"Except to try and keep a lid on your blood pressure, and don't go haywire. Justice hasn't even been indicted yet."

"Will they do that?"

"That's up to Judge Gleason. If there's enough solid evidence against the defendant, then he has to stand trial."

"What's this country coming to?"

"If you'd listen, I'll be happy to explain just what's happening, in the legal sense."

Flopping down into one of our porch chairs, Mrs. Bly began to fan her face with a hanky. She rocked once and then quit.

"Legal, my rump. There's precious little that you'd call *legal* when you see a good man like Justice Lion come to grief . . . over some tomfool law that nobody ever needed or wanted. I'd like to grab that Volstead gink and wring his neck."

"Petunia," said Father, "so would I."

"So help me, if I as much as meet that Sternlock on any street in Liberty, I'm going to . . ."

Mrs. Bly couldn't finish her sentence. The handkerchief that had been used to fan her face now covered her mouth, and her eyes were filling.

Father knelt, patting her hand. "There now, let out a tear or two, and you'll feel better."

"No . . . I . . . won't."

"We're all incensed. Muncie and I both are, and so is Henry Gleason, so he tells me. But that's off the record, Petunia. Judge Gleason's hands are tied."

"Jail," sobbed Mrs. Bly. "They're all talking about prison. Every soul in town says the Feds are out to make an example out of Justice, to spook the rest of us. That's what they say."

"Easy now, Petunia. As you know, dear lady, we all say more than our prayers. It's my guess that Justice may have to pay a small fine. . . ."

"Times are hard, Jesse. And the Lions have to eat, just like all of us. It's not fair, taking money out of Justice Lion's pocket, just so some government cop can goose himself a promotion."

"I want to go see," I told my father.

"Go ahead, but take care, Muncie. I don't want you involved in any of this, hear?"

"I hear."

Running down the slate sidewalk and into town, I caught up with the focal point of the activity, where Justice Lion was just reaching the jail. Rake Tatum was there, standing in the doorway; leaning, as usual, on his cane. I got as close as I could. Mr. Sternlock was there, too.

"I'm here, Sheriff."

Rake Tatum said, "I'm sorry, Justice, but it's my sworn duty to tell you that you're under arrest."

"You said so yesterday."

"Yup, so I did."

Justice Lion said, "I'm beholding to you, Rake. Like I spoke yesterday, I needed one day's time to settle my wife . . and charge Hem, my son, to head the household until I return."

I saw Mr. Tatum's hand reach up on his shirt to touch his star, his sheriff's badge. One of the tips pointed straight up. He wasn't liking his job very much, I imagined; not when he had to arrest a friend.

"Thank you, Justice."

Right then I looked at the face of Justice Lion, remembering all the ripe peaches that I had stolen, with Hem, from his peach tree. People stood around in clusters of twos and threes, staring at Justice Lion, as if they wanted to point a finger and whisper his name. Stared with their mouths open.

Justice Lion entered the jail. But before he walked inside, he tilt back his head and all his big shock of gray hair, to look up at the sky. One quick look, as if to pay a farewell to the outdoors, so much of which he owned. I thought about the paper that Hem had told me about, the night that we'd hunted the coon with Whelper and Blue. The paper in Justice Lion's strongbox that had been signed, centuries ago, by George Rex, the King of England . . . the document that had deeded Kipp's Mountain to the Lions.

Someday, I hoped, Uncle Justice would sign over Kipp's Mountain, in one way or another, to Hem.

Closing my eyes, I envisioned the figure of Justice Lion as he had paraded down the main street. Every step that he'd taken on the brown gravel road, wearing dusty black shoes, with no laces, and no stockings. Just his thick white ankles, unclad, beneath the fraying cuffs of his trousers. To some, perhaps, he had looked shabby, like a secondhand citizen.

Not to me. I felt like hollering out to the whole town that there was the man who allows me, Muncie Bolt, to call him Uncle Justice, and there should have been a color guard, or a flag, just to welcome him back into Liberty.

I had the urge to run uphill, up to the mountain, to see Hem and Blessing. Shake the hand of Hem Lion and then hug and kiss his sister. Hem wants to wed that gal named May and I want to marry Blessing, and be alone with her, all night. Every night for the rest of my life. I wish I could have her picture, the way Father kept a photograph of my mother.

What could I do now, about Justice? I looked down at the dirt of the road, walking back to our house, wondering how Father could help. Well, at least I knew he would take some sort of action, and not just tarry idle to let Justice go to prison.

Picking up a fallen maple twig, I ran it along Mrs. Ortengren's white picket fence, making a tut-tut-tut noise. Mrs. Ortengren was a real nice lady who would, on occasion, bring a pie over to my father and me. She'd asked me not to rattle her fence, several times. I don't know why I was doing it now. Maybe I just wanted to get even with somebody, or hurt something.

I felt mean.

Just as I got home, to turn in at our front gate, I saw someone coming out of our front door, Judge Henry Gleason. I hadn't seen him up close in over a year, maybe longer. It was hard to believe that I was now about as tall, or taller, than he was.

"Hello there, Muncie."

"Hi, Mr. Gleason. How are you?"

"Fine, lad, just fine. Busier than all get out, these days. Enjoying your summer vacation?"

"Yes, sir. By the way, congratulations. I hear you're the new county judge."

Judge Gleason nodded. "They couldn't dig up anybody else, so I guess I'll just have to grow to fit the robe."

He hurried down our walk, out the gate, and turned toward the center of town. A skinny little shrimp of a man, about seventy years old, I estimated. Older than Father. I never had quite determined if my father and Henry Gleason were friends, or enemies. Maybe they were just two lawyers in one small town.

Entering, I yelled, "Hey, I'm home."

Father was in the kitchen, brewing himself a noonday cup of tea.

"I just saw Judge Gleason," I said.

"So you did."

"You know, he hasn't been around here, at our house, in quite a while. Has he?"

"No," my father said, "he hasn't."

"How come he came today?"

"Legal business. His visit was not social, but professional."

I sat down in a kitchen chair and moved the salt cellar along the table, clinking it against the pepper. "What did he want?"

Father sighed. "Well, for one thing, he smells one powerful stink of upcoming trouble, as do I. Henry's examined the facts of the arrest of Justice Lion, and says there's no way around an immediate indictment."

"No!"

"I'm afraid so, son."

"Then what?"

"Well, then he wants to prevent trouble and no delays. A quick trial. Funny, but Henry talks like he's still the D.A."

"Do you agree with what he says?"

"In part. But I haven't told you all of it." He sat down, slowly stirring his cup of tea.

"Okay, tell me."

"Judge Gleason has appointed me as the temporary district attorney."

"Hey . . . congratulations."

"Thank you, son. But I want you to understand what this amounts to. Being the D.A. is what I've sort of wanted, you know."

"I know."

"But now it means that I prosecute Justice Lion."

Chapter 13 ❧

A law book was open.

 Father had gone over to the courthouse, saying that he'd be back in a few minutes, for supper. Earlier, he had spent most of the afternoon in his study, in shirtsleeves, looking up information and making notes on a long yellow pad. On his desk, the book that I noticed was *General Laws of Vermont,* bound in tan calfskin. It appeared to be newer than many of the other volumes that he kept in his office.

I started to read Chapter 279, which was all about the Prohibition Law of Vermont. A green slip of paper marked Section 6558:

> A person who manufactures, sells, barters, transports, imports, exports, delivers, prescribes, possesses, or furnishes any intoxicating liquor, except as authorized in this chapter, or possesses a still or other apparatus for the manufacture of intoxicating liquor, or who exposes or keeps with intent to furnish or sell intoxicating liquors, shall be imprisoned not more than 12 months, nor less than 3 months, or fined not more than $1,000 nor less than $300, or both.

Again I read the penalty paragraph.

"That's it," I said aloud.

Sitting down in Father's chair, I put my feet up on the edge of the desk, and leaned back, trying to absorb as much as I could understand about the state liquor laws. Like always, the wording was too dry and too lengthy to be very interesting. Whoever wrote it sure did enjoy saying the same things over and over.

I heard the front door.

"Is that you?" I said.

"Only me," said my father. Entering the study, he looked at my feet on his desk. "Are you expecting someone more colorful?"

"Nope."

"Reading up on Vermont law?"

"Trying to. A lot of it is confusing."

"Indeed it is, son. Without such cloudy lingo, there would be little use for all us lawyers who bicker on how the law should be interpreted."

"Sounds a bit wasteful."

"Perhaps so. Years ago, when I started reading the law, my thoughts were the same. More jargon than sense."

"How come they do that?"

"Self-preservation. Doctors and druggists do the same thing with prescriptions, to insure the layman's confusion, and ergo, his sustained dependence. Architects and builders do likewise with their blueprints, as do the fellows who survey property. Cartography, construction, and law sort of drift along in parallel lanes."

Father sat on the edge of the desk, looking at the book I was holding, as I marked Section 6558 with the tip of my finger.

"I was looking up the penalty," I said. "I guess you were, too."

"Yes, I was. Among other things."

"Can they put Uncle Justice in prison for a whole year?"

"By law, yes."

"Wow."

"However, I doubt it will come to that. You're a mite worried about all this, aren't you, Muncie?"

I nodded.

"So am I, son."

"How come you took the job?"

"I was pressured."

"You mean by Judge Gleason?"

"This is confidential, son. You are not to repeat what I'm about to tell you."

"I won't."

"Henry Gleason knew I wanted the job. Perhaps, though I'm not thoroughly positive, Henry hung onto it just so I wouldn't get it. Between you and me. But now the Feds are leaning on Henry and the pressure doesn't stop there. Some of it trickles down on my head, and from me to Justice Lion, and a trial."

"You know, I bet all this pressure you're talking about started when Elmer Sternlock came to town."

Father smiled without enjoying it. "Not quite. Someone in the Treasury Department in Washington, a whole bunch of some-bodies, put the bite on Sternlock. They want more than a smashed whiskey still."

"You mean a conviction."

"So I fear."

"And it's your job to convict."

"Well, not quite."

"Judge Gleason's then."

"No, that's not the way our courts are designed to function. Judges hear the case to apply matters of law. Matters of fact, like evidence, are sifted by a jury. And it is twelve men good and true who shall determine whether Justice Lion is convicted, or released."

"Are you going to try real hard to prosecute him?"

Father stroked his chin with a lean hand. "Yes, I'm going to try my hardest."

"I don't believe it."

"That's the way of it, son. Each side tries its level best. The law itself deserves a hearing, same as the defendant."

"But the defendant is a person. A human being. This *law* stuff is just a lot of words in a book."

Father sighed. "Funny, but I've been the acting D.A. now for only a few hours. Just since noon. Yet I already feel an obligation to the state and to the people of Vermont."

My eyes felt warm. "Justice is one of those people, in case you've forgotten."

My father slowly nodded. "Alas, so he be. Curse the timing of all this. Of all the cases to cut my teeth on, it would have to be the State of Vermont versus Justice Lion."

"Will the trial be here in Liberty?"

"Of course. As it so happens, our town is located near the center of Addison County, which determined the location of the county courthouse."

"Maybe you could disqualify yourself, and tell Judge Gleason that you don't want to prosecute just yet."

"No, I'm afraid Henry Gleason's not about to let me off the hook. He knows me as well as I know him."

"That doesn't explain much."

"Muncie, please allow me to clear up a few matters that I have, perhaps in error, shielded from you. I am in debt. This house is heavily mortgaged. For years now, my practice hasn't been as prosperous as it was before your mother died."

"We're not poor."

"Yes. We're stone broke. Not so down and out that we'll have to worry from where our next meal is coming. But I have bills in this desk that are unpaid. And we sure as shooting don't own this house."

"Who owns it?"

"The bank. Some years I manage to pay the interest on the loan, but precious little more. I guess I've been a failure." He slumped into a chair and let out a long sigh.

"You're telling me that being the new D.A. is the chance you need to dig out from under?"

"Right. This is my one opportunity, lad. Maybe it's my last chance to wipe my slate clean, own my home, educate my child. . . ."

"I'll get a job. They're looking for men over at the saw mill. I'd quit school and help out. Honest."

"Thank you, Muncie." He touched my face with the back of his hand, a gesture that he hadn't used in quite some time. "But I can't let you do that. This family is *my* responsibility, you see, and not yours."

"Yours and mine."

"Agreed. I shall retreat a step."

Jumping up, I looked out the window at Liberty. "I'd do anything to help, as long as you don't have to eat crow."

"You are distressed that I've had to compromise myself, is that it?"

I turned to face him. "In a way."

"Sometimes we all have to, lad, at one time or another. This is my time, my hour. I'm going to do it, Muncie, even though the task is more than moderately distasteful."

"What you're doing is wrong."

"Plenty of people in Liberty are going to agree with you on that score. Not all. There are more than just a handful of the self-righteous churchy will clap me on the back and salute me for cleaning up the town."

"The temperance folks."

"Yes. As I weigh the sidelines, Liberty is going to be divided down the middle. And it is not going to be pleasant. I don't relish imagining what may happen."

His eyes looked cold as he spoke. And his face was drawn, as if drained of life, empty. Maybe he knew I was sore at him. I was sure enough trying not to blame my father for what was happening.

"Muncie, when I used the word *pressure* a few moments ago, it wasn't the whole truth. Perhaps I'm using external pressure to excuse my personal reasons for wanting to be a district attorney." His hands cupped his knees as though he wanted to get up and run away.

"I'm trying to understand. But it's not very doggone easy."

"Not for you nor for me. Yet I understand myself, son, and I'm willing to own up to my ambition. It really isn't greed. I'm not trying to amass a fortune at the expense of Justice Lion."

"Well, I just counted on your defending him, and standing up for him in court. If not defending him, maybe being a character witness on his behalf."

"Gladly I would have. How I regret not walking into the street this noon and telling Justice that I'd defend him."

I scowled at Father. "Why didn't you?"

"Because when you're an attorney, you can't chase a prospective client with a butterfly net. It just wouldn't be ethical."

"Justice Lion's going to prison isn't so high-horse ethical. As I see it, a year in jail is a whole lot worse than a lawyer flagging down somebody who's in trouble and needs counsel."

"I agree. Philosophically, lad, you have me on the run."

"That's what I mean," I said. "What happens to good people is more important than ethics, or *law*." My fist hammered his desk.

"Indeed it is."

"So now you're the acting D.A."

"And I've got to get to work."

I hope you *lose,* I was thinking. But I couldn't make such a remark to my father.

"If only you were prosecuting some dirty murderer," I told him. "Boy, would I be rooting for you."

"Muncie, I won't ask you to root for me at all. I'm alone in this. Totally alone, because the people in Liberty who want Justice Lion behind bars for stilling whiskey are the only folks who will be in my corner. Ironically, I have never stood in their corner."

"No, you're not a white ribbon."

Father shook his head. "Never have been, and I don't expect I'll convert."

"You're on the wrong side. Can't you *see* that?"

"Possibly. Though I can understand that my son views the matter thus. I don't want us to be on opposite teams."

My fists came up to rest on my hips. "We are now."

"Odd. I never played on a team. When I was your age, I read books and took violin lessons, because I was so clumsy at baseball. Couldn't catch cold. And I was far too frail to play football. Oh, how I envied the boys who did, and secretly worshipped the girls who cheered for them."

"Not every kid's an athlete."

"You're right, son. And I sure wasn't. Yet I always enjoyed certain games, like checkers or chess, and poker. Games that didn't ask me to get my head bashed in or my neck busted."

"Maybe that's why you took to the law."

Father pretended to punch my knee. "Yes, that is exactly why. Perhaps I so desperately wanted to compete, and win."

"You won lots of cases."

"Lots. And lost, too. But I always went down swinging, because I gave my client all that was in me. Every ploy I knew. Which means, that now I'm the prosecutor, I intend to fill Henry Gleason's shoes, and give the defendant both barrels."

Looking at me, he read my scowl; knowing, as he so often did, just what my thoughts were. I guess he knew that I didn't hate him, but I sure hated what he was about to do.

"Son, both you and I are between the rock and the hard place."

"We sure are."

"How pleased I am to observe all the loyalty that you hold in your heart for Hem Lion's dad. And, on the other side of the coin, how sorely you are grieved that your zeal in the matter will cut me. This pleases me less."

"I guess we're on different sides, sort of like the story I read about two boys who were cousins, back in the Civil War. One in a gray uniform and the other in blue."

"How I hope, son, that you'll learn one lesson from this case."

"What is it?"

"How to disagree without being disagreeable."

What he said made me smile. Even now, the way my father said things made me admire him. He sure turned out to be a lot more than just a baseball player. A few Sundays back, I'd seen our town shortstop, Clyde Sheer, throw his bat when the ump caught him looking at a third strike. At the same pitch, my father would have swung, and hit the ball. Maybe it wouldn't go as far as when Clyde hit one of his homers, way out in the poison ivy by the fence; but at least, Father would have taken a cut at the ball.

"You're still my father. But I can't let you do what you're doing. Good golly, you've *never* been on the government's side. And now you are, against Justice."

"You want me to resign, and not be a district attorney. Is that it?"

"Yes. If I were you, I'd tell Judge Gleason you refuse to do it. And let him find somebody who's mean enough for the job."

"Sorry." Father stood up and faced me, looking me in the eye with a cold glance. "I took the job to do, not to run from."

"You won't quit."

"No, I won't. And if Justice Lion were on trial for homicide, I'd ask the jury to find him guilty."

"You're dodging."

"Perhaps."

"There's a big difference between killing somebody and making whiskey. The other day, you told me that you and Justice believe in the same things."

"So I did."

"Was that just more lawyer talk or did you really mean it?"

Father sighed. "Perhaps if you were older . . ."

"Hell! I'm plenty old enough to understand what's a lie and what's true. You always spout off that I'm too young for this and too young for that. Well, I'm not a baby anymore. I have feelings for Justice Lion. And for Hem, too. That's not all. I've got a whole lot of feelings for Blessing."

He squinted at me. "Blessing?"

"Yes. She's more than just pretty. I have feelings for her that are a lot more than I've ever had for anybody. . . ."

"You're becoming a man, I guess."

"Reckon so."

"More than I was aware of. And here I thought that you were gallivanting up to the hills to hunt coon with Hem."

"That part of it is true. And more. Sometimes I see Blessing, and we're alone with each other. On days when I don't see her, there's sort of a hurt in me, that I can't explain."

"No need to. A man doesn't have to list his reasons for loving a woman. Or spell it all out. There are no words for love, Muncie. Poets try and fail, like parents."

"I feel like I'm going to lose something, or somebody . . . like Hem and Justice and Blessing . . . as if a piece of my heart's being torn away. And it's your fault."

My eyes were hot. I wanted to double up my fist and hit something, and hate.

Chapter 14 ❧

"Go away."

"I can't," I told Blessing.

"You best leave, Muncie."

"Maybe I would, but I don't have any place to go. Back home, on our kitchen table, I left my father a note, to tell him that I was going to run away. And never come back for a long time."

Inside my blanket roll, I'd packed some spare clothes, and a few apples. My pocket carried two dollars and seventeen cents.

"You belong in Liberty. Not up here."

"Wrong."

"Hem told me. He said your pa's on the law side. Mama knows, too. All of us Lions know. The Bolts are against us."

"Not me. Only my father."

Blessing Lion stood in a clump of young birches, her hands holding to the lean trunks, as her fingers seemed to want to tear away the loose curls of white bark.

"My pa's in your jail. And *your* pa's going to face up against him at the courthouse. You say that's not true?"

"It's true."

Dropping my gear, I walked toward Blessing, expecting her to turn and run. But she stayed among the trunks of white birches.

"I'm not a liar, Blessing."

"I know that."

"Father didn't want the job. Judge Gleason made him take it. We're broke, and that's why he accepted. Even so, my father's wrong. Money's not that important. If it is, then I hope I live poor forever."

"You won't."

"How do you know?"

"You're a Bolt. Your daddy's a big important lawyer down in Liberty and we all know it, up here."

I laughed. There wasn't any fun in my ribs. Only hurt. "That's what people think, maybe."

"Best you don't turn on your own pa. I fix to stand by mine. So does Hem."

"So I figure."

"It'd be a sorry thing if you was to turn your back to family. I'm a Lion, and I know what side I'm on, even if you don't."

"Well, it isn't that all-fired simple."

"Yes it be. Lions are all for Justice Lion, and you Bolts are against us." As she spoke, her foot stamped the earth.

Coming closer, I leaned my chest against one of the birches, looking at her face. I could see Justice and Hem and Dolly, her mother. Her face was all family.

"I sort of half hate my father."

"Don't. Best you Bolts cling fast to what you belong to, you and your town and your big courthouse. And your jail. I saw my father yesterday evening."

"You came down to Liberty."

"Yes, me and Mama and Hem. Walked into the jailhouse to see Pa."

"I hope he's okay."

"He's sick."

"No."

"Pa don't admit to it but his eyes bear him false. He never lived in a place that don't have dirt to stand on. Like our cabin. My daddy always stood on his own dirt, under his own roof, eating food he raised himself. Not storebought. He won't eat."

"Sure he will . . . if he gets hungry. Your dad's got a big appetite."

"I saw his arms reach through the bars and hold Mama, and me, and then Hem. Like we'd got tore out of him. He's a man in dark water, grabbing."

"Did he cry?"

"No, but I did. Mama, too. But not Hem. All he done was kick the bars with his boot, until Rake Tatum come back, and then Pa told Hem to rest easy."

"I'm sorry, Blessing."

"No need to bother. It isn't your fault. But it'll be your pa's fault if he wins against Justice. His doing."

As I tried to touch Blessing's hand, slowly, she slid hers away. I didn't try again. So all I did was lean on the birch and think of the right words to say.

"The trial's tomorrow."

"We know. All us Lions'll come. We got a right to be heard and stand by Justice. We got rights to earn a living, same as lawyers and judges and Fed men."

"You sure do."

"My pa bought the copper with garden money, the metal for his still. He didn't steal it. And he bought the sugar, too. Planted his own sweet corn. Why can't folks let us live lonesome?"

"My father would nod to all that."

"He's foreign now, Hem says. You and your pa are friends to us no longer."

I shook, feeling sort of dizzy inside my stomach. "I suppose Hem feels that way. The night we went after catfish, in the boat, Hem was my pal . . . until we saw Mr. Sternlock and Rake Tatum, on horses. Then he turned on me like a toothy dog."

"Hem's no dog."

"I didn't mean that."

"My brother's a coydog. Because his face is so sweet, he may look to some folks like a farmdog that brings in cows. But he's as free as any wild coy that ever barked a moon."

"That's how I want to live, Blessing. Sort of like Hem. I've wanted to be like Hem for so long I can't even remember when the wish got born."

"Hem doesn't want to be you."

I felt the cut of it, and it hurt. Worse, I knew she was right. Hem was always so happy just being Hem, until now.

I said, "I don't much want to be me, either."

Her hand touched mine. "I'm sorry, Muncie. I can read the sorry in your eyes, like what's in Justice's eyes, and Mama's. But I just had to tell you what I see in Hem."

"What do you see?"

"Hem's coiling. We can't see his fangs. His talk is low and deep, near to a whisper, when he says anything to any of us. He's so gentle with Mama, and me, that us womenfolk hardly know it's Hem."

"I like your brother, Blessing."

"Well, I never took to Hem a whole lot. Until recent. Justice used to give Hem a real tanner, whenever he'd act up raw. Hem's not raw no longer."

"How's he taking it?"

"Hem's ripe. His back spine is straight up tall, but inside, it's arched up stiffer than a cornered cat. Last evening, late, when we'd walked clear home from the jail, Hem snuck into Mama's bed . . . and sung her to sleep."

So many feelings boiled up in me. I felt like shouting or crying. It was all I could do to hold it all back.

"He held Mama in his arms, like you'd cradle a baby, and rocked her. Singing sweet. Delicate as a lark's call."

"Please tell Hem I'm still his pal."

"Wouldn't prosper you much if I did. Hem goes his own way, Justice says. Them two fight like two rats in a sack. Leastwise, they used to. Will again as soon as Justice serves his jail time."

"Nobody knows how it'll turn out."

"Except for my pa. He knows."

"How does he?"

Before answering, Blessing took my hand and led me to a flat gray rock. Beside the stone, some late black-eyed Susans were growing. I counted six blossoms, with buttons dark as chocolate, and buttery petals.

"Papa just knows. Never said as much to any of us, last evening, but I know he already seed the outcome. Like he's viewing the sundown sky and knows it'll soon be dark."

"I wish you wouldn't say things that way."

"Papa and Mama raised us, Hem and me, to look Liberty in the eye, and not bow down. To see the straight of it and not double under, even if what we see is a bitter broth."

"I guess you're plenty worried," I said.

"Not over Justice. He'll hold."

"Who over?"

"Mama and I are worried about Hem."

"Hem?"

"What he'll do. How he'll take it if his pa gets the prison sentence. Justice understands more of Liberty law than he lets on. But not Hem. My brother is a law himself."

"They should have let Justice come home until the trial," I said.

"Pa said no. Said he'd not raise a penny of bail money for fear he'd startle and run off, and it would forfeit. Some of my uncles were ready to put up, but Pa said no. He told us all to keep the silver in the kist."

"What's a kist?"

Blessing smiled softly. "Nothing to do with kissing. A kist is just a money store, a home bank. We all got silver and gold. Not much, but ours. Justice squirrels it away, for the rainy future, he says."

"That makes sense." As I spoke, I thought about Father and his debts, his messy old desk with unpaid bills inside. Once I found myself a job, I'd send my two dollars back to him in my first letter, even though the money was mine. I'd earned it.

Blessing said, "We got gold pieces . . . twenty-dollar, ten, five . . . and some two-and-half. Part will go to Hem one day, and the other half for my dowry."

If I marry you, I wanted to tell Blessing, you won't need a dowry. I'll be all you'll ever have reason to want. As I thought to myself Blessing Lion looked at me, softly.

"Someday," she said, "when it's over."

Her arms went around my neck, and her face touched my cheek. I was hoping that she'd cry, because I wanted to so badly. All I did was hold her tight, and hang on. I felt like I was in some sort of a war that I didn't want to fight, and both sides were losing. Miss Kimberly, a teacher at school, said that both armies always lose. There were no winners in a war.

"It's all wrong, Blessing. My father wants to win and I want him to lose. But he respects your father. So do I."

"Used to be."

"Everything's changed. I'm hanging upside down, like a bat, and I hate it all. Down in Liberty, everybody's starting to disrespect everyone else."

I thought about Mrs. Bly, and how loyal she always was to my father. Soon she'd know about his being the new District Attorney, prosecuting Justice Lion . . . and hate my father for doing it.

"I hate him, too," I said.

Blessing looked at me, confused.

"Damn it, I hate what my father is doing to me, to himself, and to Uncle Justice. I just don't see how he could do their dirty work. We need the money. Maybe that's why. God, there's got to be a reason all this is happening."

"Papa says there's a reason for all that's natural. But the laws of Liberty are town-made and no mountain man is bred to knuckle under."

"I saw some old newspaper pictures of the World War, in Europe, with some big high rows of barbed wire. Maybe that's what Vermont ought to have. Some walls of barbed wire that would keep the people in Liberty apart from the uphillers."

"Papa doesn't hold any with fences. Never did."

"He's a good man, your old pa."

"Real gentle. A lot like you, Muncie."

"No, I could never hope to be anything as strong as Justice, or Hem."

"Which side of the barbed wire are *we* on?"

"I'm so mixed up, I'm not on any side at all. Just caught in the middle of it, I guess. Like being ripped up into hunks."

"Papa told us about a calf that'd got herself caught in barbed wire. All tore up, the poor thing. Had to shoot it dead."

"Please," I begged Blessing, "let's not talk about death and dying. I can't abide it." Reaching down with my hand, I touched the petals of a black-eyed Susan, not wanting to pick it. Or uproot it. All I wanted was to see the blossoms live forever.

"Muncie, where'll you go to?"

"I don't yet know. Maybe I was sort of wishing that you and your ma, and Hem, would take me in, so I could work my keep."

Blessing Lion looked at me, touching my face ever so gently with the tips of her fingers, stroking my hair. "If you and I were of age . . ."

"Soon we will be. I guess our feelings have already come of age, in ways."

She nodded. "They rightful have."

"All I want to do is wrap my arms around you and just hold on for always."

"That's a runaway."

"Yes, I reckon it is," I said.

"And right now is no time to run. Not for you, and not for me, because your pa needs you like Justice needs all us Lions."

Blessing sounded so solid, so loyal, that it made me feel like hiding my face. Or crawling under the rock upon which we sat. I wanted to squirm into a ball, in my own bed back home, down inside the covers where the eyes of Vermont couldn't stare my way.

I remembered the note I'd written:

Dear Father,
Goodbye. I can't take living in Liberty any longer, watching you send Justice to prison. Don't worry about me because I'll

get a job. And write to you. Maybe things will be easier if you don't have me to feed. I'm sorry I turned out so rotten, and I don't guess I'm worthy enough to be a minister. Or to even be your son.

Muncie

"You're atremble."

"Guess I got the shakes," I said, trying to steady one of my hands with the other. I didn't relish having Blessing take notice of how I was coming apart. Lifting my palms up to my face, I tried to burrow into the sudden darkness.

Blessing held me. Her arms were around me, drawing close; and she began to hum softly into my ear. Even so, I felt cold.

"Remember?" she said. "In school, just last year, right after Miss Hubbard took her trip to Boston, and she told us about a manuscript she read that got writ by a man called Melville?"

"I recall."

"The story was called *Billy Budd*. And while she told us about it, in school when she talked about Billy, I always thought about you. In all of my daydreams, Billy Budd's face was always yours, Muncie."

"Honest?"

"His smile was your smile."

"I liked the way Miss Hubbard told us that story. Even though it was sad."

"Someday," said Blessing, "she said it was going to be a book, for everybody to read. And when I get to read it, I hope there aren't no pictures inside. Because I want to see your face in that Billy boy."

Listening to Blessing, I thought about school, and how it would be starting in two weeks, early September. I didn't want to run away.

"Look," she said. "Here's more Susans behind the rock."

I looked. "They're old. All gone to seed. No more yellow petals. Just dried up and wilted brown." I didn't want to see anything dead.

"That's their way."

Leaning over, Blessing snapped off a fawn-colored head, holding the dry husk, that had once been the center of color, in her hand. With her fingernail, she picked apart the sharp prongs, opening the husk.

"See?"

"I don't see much, except chaff."

"These wee slivers are seeds. Black, tipped with silver." She blew away the brown husks, leaving the seeds to lie in her white palm.

"Okay," I said. "They're seeds."

"Come," she said.

Pulling me up from the rock, Blessing led me to a nearby spot, in sunlight, where the black earth was soft and wet. Bending, she dug small pockets into the dirt, carefully depositing a seed into all but one.

"I hope they spring up beautiful," I said. "Like you, Blessing."

Her hand touched her belly. "Years from now I'll grow life in me. New baby life, and from your seed. Flowers to cry in the night for my breast."

Watching her hand slowly climb up her own body, from her belly to her breasts, I wanted to touch her. I wanted to be all of Blessing Lion and to have her be all of me. And for the two of us to be one seed.

"My babe," she said, "boy or girl, will never leave from you, Muncie. Never will my baby turn its back to its father."

Blessing drifted into the trees.

Chapter 15 ∂∾

"All rise."

"A ll rise."
Chairs and benches all groaned, as every citizen in the packed courtroom stood up, with due respect. From the back row, all I could see was a herd of hairy heads. A few of the women wore bonnets, and flowered hats. The men were bare-headed, and a shaggy number hadn't made too recent a trip to Zack Welling's barbershop.

Up front, on the opposite side of the bench from the witness box, I saw Mrs. Harp who taught shorthand to the girls at our high school. She wore a gray dress, with a white collar, and in her lap was a stenography pad.

Judge Henry Gleason entered, from up front, dressed in a robe the color of coal that was a bit too long for such a short man. Holding it up, he climbed the stairs, to occupy the highback chair behind the bench.

"Hear ye, hear ye . . ." Rake Tatum's nasal voice made a sharp echo in the courtroom. "The County Court of Addison County in the State of Vermont is hereby now declared in session."

Henry Gleason rapped his gavel. "Please be seated."

We all sat. Several people resumed their earlier conversations in low whispers which faded into a tense silence.

Rake Tatum said, "People versus Justice Lion."

Sheriff Tatum took his seat, back to the audience, and beside his prisoner, the broad back of Justice Lion.

"Do the people have counsel present?" Gleason asked.

My father rose. "They do, your honor. My name is Jesse Bolt."

"Defense?"

A young man in a dark blue suit stood to answer. He'd been sitting beside Justice. "Yes, your honor. My name is Miles Harvey, appointed by this court to counsel the defendant."

Justice Lion's deep voice growled out, "I got no need for a lawyer."

"Order," snorted Judge Gleason. "If the defendant wishes to be heard on his own behalf, such opportunity will be subsequently provided. Counsel for defense is instructed to maintain his client's silence until such time."

"Yes, your honor."

I had never met Miles Harvey, but I knew that he was new in the county, from up in Stillwell, as Father had once mentioned his name. He looked very young and sort of fresh-hatched. He patted down his hair, as though unsure of what to do next; and it was obvious to see why he'd been appointed by the court. To lose.

"People will state their case," said Gleason.

Father stood up. "Your honor, the people intend to prove that Justice Lion, the defendant, wantonly and knowingly, manufactured illicit alcoholic beverage . . ." half of the audience quietly tittered ". . . and was in the process of such activity when apprehended by both federal and local authority."

"Plea to charges?"

Miles Harvey stood. "Innocent, your honor."

An open aisle, about two chairs wide, divided the courtroom congregation. Sitting to the left were townfolk, people I knew. On the right, behind Justice, were the uphillers, the Lions, poorly dressed, statue still on their hard seats, as if strange to such confinement of so many people inside one building.

Behind me, several people were standing, leaning against the rear wall. I was aware that I sat on the Lion side of the room, not behind Father. In a way I wanted to sit on both sides. Not wishing to be seen, I didn't sit up very tall, but hunkered down.

Last night, I had not gone home. Even though I'd sneaked back and had seen a light burning in Father's study. He had been preparing, as always. But I just couldn't make myself crawl back, so I had stayed with the Blys. I had slept in a bed between two of the youngest Bly boys. It sure wasn't very restful.

Four or five rows in front of me, I spotted Petunia Bly, on the Lion side of the crowd. For once, she wasn't talking.

"People may proceed."

Father had remained on his feet. Turning, he faced the jury of twelve men. None of the twelve, I noticed, were uphillers. Justice's young lawyer, Miles Harvey, never should have agreed to such a one-sided jury. Half of the jury, I was thinking, ought to be Lions . . . or at least some uproad people. I remembered what Father had said when telling me about the trial of Drury Lion, and how my father had carefully drawn the jury.

Well, he'd done it again. Only now, the jury would be stacked against the Lions. In the jury box, I recognized three elders of the Methodist Church here in Liberty. White ribbon guys. And a few more professed teetotalers. Among the jury, there were no men that my father had ever played poker with, or even mentioned.

It was going to be a hot August day. I loosened one of the top buttons of my shirt in order to free my collar.

"The people call Mr. Elmer Sternlock."

Father's words were followed by the immediate rise of Elmer Sternlock from the front row of the courtroom. His body appeared extra beefy as he faced lanky Rake Tatum who held out a black Bible. Sternlock's left hand touched it.

"Do you swear by Almighty God," said Sheriff Tatum in a monotone, "that the testimony you shall give be the truth, the whole truth, and nothing but the truth?"

"I so swear."

"Be seated."

Mr. Sternlock's bulk filled the witness box as he took his seat.

Father said, "Sir, please state your name."

"Elmer Sternlock."

"And how are you employed?"

"I am a salaried agent in the Federal Bureau of Prohibition of the Treasury Department of the United States Government."

"Have you come to the community of Liberty, Vermont, to serve in such official capacity?"

"I have."

"And were you performing said duties on the twentieth day of August of this year, 1923?"

"Yes, I was."

"What specifically were, or are, your assigned duties?"

"As a federal agent, I am responsible to investigate, detect, and arrest all persons who engage in the manufacture, traffic, and marketing of illicit whiskey."

The crowd growled.

"This is your specialty?"

Sternlock nodded his head. "It is."

"On that day, twenty August, did you in fact execute your duty?"

"Yes."

"Were you alone?"

"No, I was accompanied by your local officer."

"Your companion's name, please."

"Sheriff Tatum, right over there." Sternlock nodded toward Rake who had taken his seat once again beside Justice. People in the audience shook their heads as if in disbelief.

"Just the two of you?"

"Well, I suppose so," snorted Sternlock, "unless you want to throw in two horses and a pig."

The crowd exploded a laugh. Judge Gleason also smiled, yet raising his gavel in a gesture that warned all visitors to settle down.

Elmer Sternlock glared at Rake Tatum. "The pig, I must add, was not *my* idea. She belongs to your local expert."

"By that, you mean the sow in question is the sole property of Sheriff Tatum?" Father smiled.

"Yes."

Gleason rapped his gavel. "Counsel will please move along. I believe the jury and the court have now assumed that Rake's personal property is indeed swine . . . and not a federal marshal."

The audience loved it. But the sudden red on Elmer Sternlock's face indicated a deeper emotion. He muttered something which I couldn't hear, glowering at Henry Gleason.

"Objection, your honor."

From the bench, our new county judge looked over his halfmoon glasses, reacting to Miles Harvey's outburst.

"I object on the grounds that Mr. Sternlock has just become a hostile witness."

"Well now," said Henry Gleason, "I believe that the witness is perhaps hostile to the court, for improper humor, and to Rake's animal . . . but not in any way toward your client or his cause. Overruled."

Father said, "Mr. Sternlock, exactly where did you and Sheriff Tatum go, on horseback, on the established day?"

"All over Hell's half acre."

Judge Gleason rapped away the laughter.

"Would you care to be more precise?"

"Huh. We followed that dang pig of his up every ravine and down into every gully and swamp this side of Perdition. All I know is that we were up on what is locally known as Kipp's Mountain."

"Shall we narrow that a bit for the jury? I take it," my father said, "that you were more or less in the vicinity of where the defendant resides."

"Objection."

"Sustained," grunted Henry Gleason. "Jesse, you know better than to lead a witness along by his nose."

"Excuse me, your honor. Now, Mr. Sternlock, where exactly were you?"

"Up on Kipp's Mountain. I'd say less than three miles due west from the center of town. At best, that's a guess."

"Tell us, please, in your own words, what you and Sheriff Tatum discovered."

"A whiskey still."

"Objection. How will the jury know that such an *alleged* apparatus was in fact found?"

Before the bench could react, Father nodded to two of Mr. Sternlock's men who then pulled off a bedsheet to uncover something. They lifted several large pieces of tarnished copper, dusty firebricks, and some tubing onto a table. Necks all craned to see.

"Sheriff Tatum," said Father, "may I please ask you to tag and mark these parts of a whiskey stilling device as Exhibit A?"

"So ordered," said Judge Gleason. "It's a still."

"Mr. Sternlock," my father continued, "are these pieces of the still that you personally discovered and destroyed?"

"They are. If you will look at the tub of that copper cooker, you will notice my initials, E.S., and the date."

"So noted."

"Describe, please, the condition of this device about the time you confiscated it."

"Hotter than Hades."

"Order," warned Gleason, smiling as he gestured.

"Other than heat, what else, if anything at all, was the still producing?"

"Corn mash whiskey. Three men were there, and maybe more, but all of them tailed off into the woods. We nabbed only one man. The one who held his ground."

"And," said Father, "is that particular gentleman that you apprehended in this courtroom?"

"Yes, he is." Sternlock leveled an arm at Justice. "We caught, and placed under arrest, the defendant, Mr. Justice Lion."

Throats growled.

"Quiet," said Henry Gleason in his scratchy voice, "or I'll empty the courtroom."

"And what happened," asked Father, "after you placed the defendant under arrest?"

Sternlock glanced at Rake Tatum. "You won't believe it. Not a doggone word of it."

Gleason said, "Witness will answer the question."

"Very well, your honor. I was about to put the cuffs on Lion when your sheriff told me to lay off. And then he asks the defendant if he will come into town the next day to the Liberty jail, and turn himself in."

Father looked at Justice. "And did he?"

Elmer Sternlock scowled. "Yes." Curling a lip as if in disgust, he added, "And if you ask me, it's a puny way to wear a badge."

Judge Gleason cleared his throat. "The court recorder will strike the witness's last remark, as we do not convene here to determine the fitness of our fellow public servants. I must remind you, Mr. Sternlock, to limit your testimony to the questions asked you by counsel."

"Sorry, your honor."

"One more question, Mr. Sternlock. Did you or Sheriff Tatum also confiscate a sample of what the defendant's alleged still was preparing?"

"Yes. Over there."

A glass mason jar was set atop the table and marked Exhibit B by Rake Tatum, after Judge Gleason and all twelve jurors were allowed a healthy sniff.

"Don't swallow it, Carl," someone in the crowd whispered too loudly, causing Henry Gleason to scowl and a juror's face, Carl Springer's, to redden.

Father turned to Miles Harvey. "I have no more questions for Mr. Sternlock at this time."

Mr. Harvey just sat still.

So my father, I guessed to be helpful, raised his eyebrows to his youthful adversary, and I read his lips when he whispered, "Cross-examine?"

"Oh," said Miles Harvey, jumping up to his feet, spilling a glass of water onto his notes. "Yes, I have one question." Then he paused for what seemed to be more than a minute. I could hear scores of ticks from the clock on the courtroom wall.

Gleason said, "Would counsel care to ask it?"

The crowd appreciated the bench's wit, and Judge Gleason enjoyed his moment of limelight. Father always said that Henry was quite a ham.

"When you and Sheriff Tatum and the pig found the alleged still, Mr. Sternlook . . ."

"Sternlock."

"Sorry. When you discovered the alleged device, were you on Mr. Lion's land?"

"Nope. We'd rode those two nags around in circles, so I'd say they wasn't as much as a broom closet within a mile of that still."

"You're certain of this, Mr. Sternlock? Even though you previously admitted that you were hopelessly lost."

All the Lions hooted.

Mr. Sternlock scowled, answering, "You know I'm a stranger in these parts. I testified we were about three miles west of town, and that's all I care to say about the location."

Judge Gleason said, "Counselor, is the exact location of import to your defense?"

"Yes, your honor, I believe so."

"May I ask why?"

For years, according to what Father told me, Henry Gleason as D.A. had enjoyed chewing green young attorneys into small pieces. He seemed about ready to add one more to his disaster list. But what happened next came as a real shocker.

"The next part of my question to the witness, your honor, may answer your question."

"Proceed."

"Mr. Sternlock . . ."

"I'm glad you finally learned his name," cackled Judge Gleason. He grinned at the jury and then yawned at the back of his hand.

"Mr. Sternlock," continued Miles Harvey, "then if you were *not* on Mr. Lion's land at the time of the arrest, may I presume that you presented a search warrant?"

The courtroom was very silent.

"No," said Sternlock. "No warrant was called for as we weren't on his land."

"Wrong."

All heads looked at Justice Lion. I suspected that Henry Gleason, from the bench, would again demand that the defendant be quiet. But he didn't. Instead he looked at my father, and then addressed Mr. Harvey.

"Does counsel wish to confer with his client?"

"Yes, your honor. Please?"

"Granted. Be brief."

I saw Miles Harvey walk over to Justice and whisper. Justice nodded, and the young attorney smiled.

"Your honor, my client informs me that all of Kipp's Mountain is Lion land."

"I don't believe it," said Sternlock.

Gleason rapped his gavel, and looked at Justice Lion's young attorney. "Any more questions to the witness?"

"No, your honor. Not at this time."

"Mr. Sternlock," said Gleason, "you may step down."

I watched Elmer Sternlock move his big sweaty frame from the witness box and retake his seat up front. He looked like a bull. Ready to gore.

Chapter 16 🐦

"Open those windows."

Judge Henry Gleason's highpitched voice quacked out his request for ventilation. The courtroom was steaming. Not a breath of air, and I saw dark clouds of sweat growing on just about every shirt, and dress.

"They won't open, Henry . . . I meant to say your honor," said a member of the jury.

"They got painted in. Stuck fast."

"I can't believe it." Coming down from the bench, almost tripping on his black robe, Judge Gleason yanked at one window after another. Nothing budged. "Dang it! Who painted this place?"

My father grinned. "I believe, your honor, the paint job was performed just last week . . . by your wife's brother."

The crowd chuckled.

"Then he's a damn fool. I can't stand this infernal monkey suit another second." Henry Gleason loosened the top buttons of his black robe. As he wasn't wearing a collar on his shirt, several of those in attendance cracked a smile.

Petunia Bly had removed one of her big shoes. As for me, even though I wasn't a participant, I was wet clean through, feeling as if I was sitting in a puddle.

Judge Gleason regained the bench. "Proceed."

Father rose. "Your honor, I call at this time, the people's second witness, Sheriff Rake Tatum."

Mrs. Harp, the court secretary, swore him in.

"Please tell the jury your name, sir."

Henry Gleason's thumb softly snapped a red suspender against his damp shirt. "God sakes, Jesse, do we have to hear all this? Everybody in town knows the witness. Let's get on with it."

"Sheriff Tatum, you were with Agent Sternlock when he arrested the defendant."

Rake Tatum nodded. "I was."

"And, to dispense with duplicating testimony, do you support the evidence given by Mr. Sternlock?"

"Depends."

Gleason looked sideways at the witness box, but did not speak.

"By this," said my father, "I conclude you wish to be refreshed in memory from the minutes."

Judge Gleason sighed and nodded.

"Yes," said Rake.

Mrs. Harp, without any excitement in her voice whatsoever, recited the questions and answers concerning Elmer Sternlock's testimony. As she read, Judge Henry Gleason's fingers drummed his desktop as though playing a fife. "Please continue, Jess."

"Sheriff, can you support the record?"

"Some of it."

"Which part can you *not* support?"

"Well," said Rake, "the part about the legal or illegal search."

"What about it?"

"Seems to me I don't recall just where the town line quits and where Kipp's Mountain begins."

"Then," said Father, "allow me to ask if *you* yourself have ever found it necessary to use a local warrant to search any defendant's home and property. What I ask you, Sheriff, is this: Have you constantly employed warrants of search while performing the duties of Addison County?"

Smelling a rat, I wondered what my father was up to. He'd often told me that a good lawyer never asks a question in court unless he's cocksure of the answer. Why was he breaking his own rule?

Maybe he was on Justice's side after all. No, that couldn't be true, as Rake Tatum's answer gave Father what he wanted.

"No, I don't never carry no search warrant. Never needed one. As you know, Jess, we got a peace-loving town."

Elmer Sternlock grunted.

"Sheriff," warned Judge Gleason, "you are a witness for the prosecution in this case, and *not*, may I instruct you, serving in the capacity of the Chamber of Commerce."

Rake said, "I apologize to the court, your honor."

"Listen," said Gleason, "I've had about as much *your honor* as I can stomach. I'm up here in this dreadful heat, not even wearing my robe, and sweating like a sundown mule. Enough of all this corny courtship, and let's get on with the trial before we all pass out."

The audience clapped.

"No more questions," said Father.

"I have no questions," said Miles Harvey, bringing a relieved expression to Judge Gleason's face, "except one. Or two."

"Proceed. Proceed."

"Is it true, Sheriff, that you allowed the defendant to return home, and then turn himself in on the following day?"

"That's the truth."

"Why, sir, did you make such a concession?"

"Because," said Rake Tatum, "I have known Justice Lion my whole life."

"Is that all?"

"And I knew that he's somebody worthy of our trust. Mr. Lion is a good citizen and an honorable man."

All the Lions in the courtroom, plus their kin and their friends in town, let out a cheer. Standing up, waving her monstrous shoe, was Petunia Bly.

"God bless ya, Rake!" she hollered. "You got *my* vote."

"Order," said Henry Gleason. "The gallery will control its deportment and not prejudice the jury in one direction or another."

Mrs. Bly sat, receiving several pats on her meaty back from those who sat nearby. One lady even stretched back, from two rows ahead, to touch her hand. It was Mrs. Milmine, who baked pies for our church.

"No more questions." Miles Harvey was smiling.

Judge Gleason asked, "Will you, Jesse, and young what's-his-name for the defense, please approach the bench?"

Mr. Harvey and my father stepped forward. For the obvious reason, the courtroom fell deadly silent, as each ear strained to catch what was none of their business. People in Liberty loved a juicy secret and told each one they knew to every other soul who would listen.

"Boys," said Henry, "we got a problem. You see . . ." The rest of what Judge Gleason told the two of them would remain a momentary mystery. Henry glanced over at the jury and then back to the two attorneys, who then resumed their seats.

"Members of the jury," said Judge Gleason, "one of you, as we all know, is Marvin Murphy. Now, it seems that Mr. Murphy is also our village clerk. So I shall now ask you, Marv, if you will excuse yourself, and go fetch the deed book."

"I can't, Henry."

"Why not?"

"Because it's in the safe."

Judge Gleason sighed. "Then open her up and please bring us the deed book. Good grief, your office is just down the hall."

"I don't know how it happened, Henry, but I somehow forgot the combination."

"You *what?*"

"You see, it's only August," said Marvin.

Gleason snapped. "What about it?"

"Tax time's in April. And mid March is usually when I open up the safe, crack the property list, and levy the taxes. I can't do it right now, because it's only August."

"Holy sweet Hannah," said Judge Gleason, "I don't believe all this. Why in Hell can't you open your stupid safe anytime you darn please?"

"Easy now, Henry," said Mr. Murphy. "No use getting all fussed up. I open her up every March, don't I?"

Wiping the sweat fog from his glasses, Judge Gleason, in a tired voice, said, "Dear, dear . . . won't you tell us why you *can't* open the safe today?"

"Well, in summer I wear my cotton suit, like I did today. And in late fall, I switch over to my wool suit, and that's where I keep the combination. In the vest of my wool suit." Mr. Murphy broke into a grin and slapped his leg. "Safe and sound."

Ignoring the joke, Judge Gleason said, "Then please get on the phone, back in my chambers, and call up your house . . . if you can remember the number . . . and tell Elizabeth to kindly *read* you the combination."

"I can't, Henry. Would if I could."

"Pete's sake, why *can't* you?"

"Elizabeth's not to home."

"Where is she?"

"Left early this morning to visit her sister, in Brattleboro. She took sick last June. The doc says it's her kidneys, but if you ask me, it just might be her liver."

Looking up, I saw Henry Gleason lay his head down on his high desk. Every mouth in the courtroom seemed to be laughing, talking, saying nothing. Even old Justice, looking back over his shoulder, was heard to be laughing. It was strange how Elizabeth Murphy's sister's ailing kidney, or liver, could tickle everybody's funnybone.

The gavel sounded.

"We shall," said Judge Gleason, "all take a recess, eat a noonday meal, and patiently wait for our village clerk to trot home and search his vest for the combination to the safe."

"All rise," said Rake Tatum.

Grabbing his black robe from the back of his chair, Judge Henry Gleason marched from our court of law.

Father was turning around, speaking to someone, and I didn't want to see him, or let him know that I'd come to watch him prosecute Justice Lion. I saw plenty of people I knew. But I couldn't locate either Hem or Blessing. We were all sort of milling around, still in two groups: Lions, and local folks. Some crowd.

Several of the Lions looked like rough characters, men I wouldn't want to meet after dark; or even in daylight, if I was up on Kipp's Mountain. Here, even in Liberty, I noticed how the Lion men and women kept to themselves. They were on enemy ground and they knew it.

Some of the town people wore white ribbons, held to a shirt or a dress by a pin, to signify that they were upholding Temperance. One of the Lion men, tall, with a thick black beard, stared at one of the white ribbons. His fist clenched, as if he was about to rip it off the chest of the man who wore it. But then he turned his back to the ribbon, his face as expressionless as granite. Except for his eyes. Lion eyes were bright, glowing, as though behind them lay embers that patiently smoldered.

"Muncie!"

Wincing when I heard my name, I turned around, but not in time to defend myself from what was close to being an attack.

Mrs. Bly's arms wrapped around me, squeezing me harder than a sow bear. She felt so warm, so wonderful, that I did my best trying to hug her, too. Petunia Bly just hugged me heavy and wouldn't let loose. I always felt that I was sort of a special kid in her life, even though she had a healthy litter of her own, so many that she could hardly remember all their names.

"You're coming home with *me*," said Mrs. Bly, "so's I can fuel you up proper."

I had told her, last night, that I'd left home, and I figured she somehow understood why. She even said that if Justice Lion got sent to prison that she would never clean our house again. Well, it wasn't our house. Maybe it will soon be the bank's house, and my father would no longer have a home. The thought turned my eyes hot. At the moment, I hated everything in the world, except Mrs. Bly.

"I won't be a burden?" I asked her.

"Burden? *You?* My stars, no. Besides, I'm built for bearing burdens. Ask old Harry, next time he's sober. Anyhow, I won't have you feeding at your pa's table. Not after today. Never, unless you prefer to. By the way, I told your pa you're safe. So's he won't worry none. Figured you'd want me to."

"It's hard to say *what* I want, Mrs. Bly. Honest, I don't guess I even know who I am or why I got born."

"I know." She hugged me once more, gently. "It's the times, boy. They'll pass."

"I sure hope so."

Together, we hurried out of the courthouse to the dirt of the road. Liberty surely was crowded. People everywhere, and all sweaty. There were plenty of horses and wagons in the shade, under the courthouse elms. A few cars.

An old mare was weighted in the sun, and Mrs. Bly moved her to a cooler spot, without asking aye-yes-or-no of anybody. She sure was a mother.

"Maybe I ought to go home."

"Suit yourself. Time will heal up what's sour betwixt you and Jesse. Meanwhile, you got yourself a home at the Blys', ever and always, until you stretch to your growth."

"Thanks. I sure am beholding."

"No need. You're family, Muncie. Both you and your pa. Even now, it's hard for me to hate Jesse Bolt. He done good by me more than once."

"I don't understand him anymore."

"Neither do I. But we can't always live another soul's life, boy. He can't rein you back, and you can't halter him."

"I know," I told her.

"Suddenly there's people in Liberty who don't speak to me, and it hurts dreadful. Ladies I grew up alongside of, sat in school with, and attended when I wed Harry. Old friends, silent as smoke. Never would I guess that a few innocent jars of white whiskey could split up a town like we all was made out of rot kindling."

I decided to eat with the Blys.

At their kitchen table it was sort of like the World War. Everybody talked, shouted or sang, reached, and stole food from every plate. Much like a game. Mr. Bly was there, too; smiling, like usual, but he didn't have too much to say. Fatherhood, I guessed, was a tiring role.

I tried to count how many of us were eating in the Bly kitchen. But because so many of the kids jumped around, it was impossible to arrive at a solid sum.

"More muffins, Muncie."

"Gee, no thanks, Mrs. Bly. I'm full up."

"Good. Hey, all you kids, you best clean up this mess before the roaches do, hear?"

"We hear."

"Yes'm," I said.

There was almost a scrap to see which Bly child could wash the most dishes. And not a one got broken. I got to dry the forks and spoons and store them away in one of the kitchen drawers.

Petunia Bly sighed. "It don't seem righteous."

Her husband looked at her, smiling, and reaching.

"Not now, Harry. And quit your pinching in front of the kids or I'll bash your brains in. I got matters on my mind."

I said, "Thank you for my meal, Mrs. Bly."

"You're more than welcome. It'd be a sorry place around here if you weren't a visitor every so often. A sorry world."

"I'll see you back at court. I just want to take a walk and sort things out in my head, if you know what I'm trying to say."

"Sure I know. Come again."

Leaving by the Blys' back door, I walked along the thick hedge; not hiding, but I wasn't exactly up for a strut in the open. Was my father home? The kitchen door was shut. As it was such a hot summer day, Father would have opened it, had he been home. I wished he were home. Because, right now, that's where I wanted both of us. Home.

Aloud, I said the word. "Home."

It melted off into the sky. And I wondered, would a spoken word travel forever and ever, to be finally heard lightyears away on a distant planet, by a funny green ear? Or do people up on Mars *see* words, and talk in music instead of an alphabet?

"There sure are," I said, "a lot of things about life that I don't yet know."

Like the mortgage on our house. Our home, but only if Father can pay up what he owes. All the bills. I didn't know we were broke, and poor. Well, I didn't care if *I* was as poor as a churchmouse, but I didn't want my father to go without.

Running wouldn't help.

I'm all he's got. Maybe it would have been okay if my mother were still living. But that's only a dream. She's dead. So what do I do? Well, sir, I just take an old piece of paper and write a lousy letter to the best dad a dumb kid like me ever had. Swell. I wonder what he was thinking when he read the note. I bet he didn't *do* anything, like call up Rake Tatum, or the state police. No, not Father. Because he'd know.

He'd have reasoned I went uproad, up on Kipp's Mountain to be with the Lions, because he knows how much fun I have up yonder. Used to have.

"Is it over?" I said out into the day.

Is everything that's good in the world coming to a rancid end? It's like Vermont's got gangrene; or maybe we're lepers, infecting each other with a disease of suspicion.

Well, it's the times. But maybe I can't wait for the times to change, because Father might not live forever. He could up and die, get kicked by a frisky horse in front of the courthouse, and never know that, no matter what else happens, I'll always want to be Muncie Bolt . . . his son.

"Father?"

Bounding up our back steps, I banged the screen door, tearing into the house, not wanting him to have to wait even one more minute.

I saw him.

He was in his study. Not working, just looking at the wall. My note was in his hand.

"I'm back."

"So I see. Welcome home."

"I'm real sorry. Honest. I hate myself but I can't hate you. Rip that note up, into bits. What did you think when you found it?"

"Well, I knew you'd be nearby, somewhere. Or come to the trial. Uproad, or with Petunia Bly. You'd be with loved ones."

"Shucks. You weren't even worried?"

"Nope. I trust your maturity and judgment, even though it may be presently difficult for you to trust mine. And tell me, son, what were *your* thoughts?"

"I pictured you alone. Here, alone in your study, and it just about busted my heart."

"Right now, Muncie, without you I'd be the most *alone* man in town."

He held out his arms. It felt so good to hold him.

Chapter 17 &

Rake Tatum again said, "All rise."

If the morning was hot in our county courtroom, the afternoon promised to be even hotter. Several of the ladies present had fans; to breeze their damp faces, and to swat uselessly at the persistent heat wave.

"If it please the court," said my father, after Judge Gleason seated himself, "the people wish to call to the stand a former member of the jury, Mr. Marvin Murphy."

Looking over at the jury box, I noticed a new juror replacing Mr. Murphy. It was Will Garson, a plumber. Or rather he used to be a plumber, years back. Now he was about ninety years old but still spry.

Rake swore in the witness, and my father requested that he state his name.

"Marv Murphy . . . Marvin. I guess you know my real name's Marvin Frederick Murphy, but folks here in . . ."

Judge Gleason sighed. His black robe was nowhere in sight, but I noticed that he had buttoned a collar onto his shirt. Leaning back in his judge's chair, his thumbs were hooked beneath his red suspenders.

"Your occupation, sir?"

"For the past fifteen years, I'm the village clerk for the town of Liberty, Vermont."

Stepping over to the exhibit table, my father held up a pale grayish-green ledger which had a maroon spine. "Mr. Murphy, are you familiar with this book that I now show to the jury?"

"I sure am."

"And will you identify it, please?"

"It's the deed book. Up-to-date record of who owns what." Mr. Murphy laughed. "And who *owes* what."

The gallery responded.

"This page, so marked by this yellow slip of paper," said my father, "indicates that the township of Liberty . . . not the village, mind you, but the *township* . . . extends, by boundary, westward from the center of our town of Liberty for a distance of ten miles."

"Yes, that's correct."

"I show this to the jury."

Twelve men all leaned forward to squint at the green ledger in Fathers' hands.

"What's it say?" hollered Will Garson. Another juror repeated, more or less, what father had read from the book, concerning the township line.

"Can you tell us, Mr. Murphy, who served as village clerk prior to *your* being elected fifteen years ago?"

"Of course I can. It was my mother, the former Maybell Arthur, may God rest her soul."

A few "Amens" whispered in the audience.

"So therefore, *you,* and because your mother was the former village clerk, are the sole expert we have in Liberty, concerning its geography. Would you say so?"

"Right. My mother served thirty-one years, and I'm proud to carry on in her footsteps. And if I'm re-elected next . . ."

The gavel rapped. "Marv, if you don't mind, the next election is two years off, and it's hotter than Dutch love up here."

"Sorry, Henry. I mean your honor."

"Proceed."

"So, being a two-generation expert," Father continued, "for, if the court will allow, a total of forty-six years, you would of course know when this township of Liberty was established."

"Sure. In 1880. That's when they decided to divvy up . . . excuse me, I mean *divide* . . . Addison County into townships, for tax purposes."

Father closed the green ledger, returning it to the table. "May I request, your honor, this book be marked Exhibit C, in evidence?"

"So ordered."

Rake Tatum tagged the book, while my father began to unfold a very large blue and white paper, holding it up for the witness to observe.

"Mr. Murphy, I presume you recognize this map of . . ."

"Objection, your honor."

"Sustained. Jesse, watch your language. Proceed."

"This paper represents *what*, Mr. Murphy?"

"It's the town map."

"Drawn by a cartographer by the name of T. Enright, as I now show to you and to the jury. Can you identify T. Enright for us, please?"

"He is my nephew, who got gassed in France during the war. Struck down in the prime of life to keep the world free for . . ."

Judge Gleason whacked his gavel, three times. "Marvin, for the sake of sanity, this isn't the Fourth of July. You're not up on the bandstand making a patriotic speech. You're in the witness stand! Counsel will proceed."

"His name, please."

Marv said, "Private Thomas Enright." As he spoke the name, Mr. Murphy turned to look over his shoulder, and salute the flag. "And thank Heaven, he's still alive, even though he left Vermont to live in Denver, away off west. Married a girl out there, name of . . ."

"Marv," said Judge Gleason softly, "thank you so much for keeping us all up to snuff on the twigs of your family tree. Let's crank her up, Jesse."

"Please indicate here, Mr. Murphy, on the map, where exactly the western border of Liberty lies."

"Here." Murphy pointed. "Yes, right here."

"Will you please use this pin I now hand you, and push the pin through the map at the precise spot. Good. Members of the jury, please note where our expert has drawn the township line."

Miles Harvey stood. "Would the district attorney please allow the defendant and his counsel to also examine the map?"

Father walked over. "Of course."

"This map's a lie!" Justice Lion's deep voice boomed out a lingering echo from up front.

"Order," said Gleason. "Counsel will restrain the defendant from further outburst."

Justice Lion said, "Expert my backside."

"Order! The defendant will be given ample time to testify on any or all evidence presented. For the moment, Mr. Lion, you will remain mute, or I shall find you in contempt."

Lion voices rumbled in the crowd.

"One question more, Mr. Murphy," said Father. "Can you stipulate that the location of the defendant's property falls inside the township? In other words, to simplify matters for *all* of us, as well as for the jury, does the defendant reside anywhere between the center of town . . . *here* . . . and where you placed the pin?"

"Well, having served as village clerk for over fifteen loyal . . ."

Gleason snorted, "Jesse . . ."

"Yes, your honor. Please be brief, Mr. Murphy. Just testify a yes or a no."

"Yes."

"No more questions, your honor."

"Defense counsel may cross-examine."

"Thank you, your honor." Miles Harvey rose. "Mr. Murphy, you say that Thomas Enright who drew this map was, or rather *is,* your nephew."

"Correct."

"And he lived right here in Liberty?"

"Yes, for over twenty-five years. Or maybe twenty-six. About that, give or take a year."

"And, as Thomas Enright's uncle, did you know your nephew well?"

"Sure did. He *lived* at our house. My nephew was single and we were all the family he had."

"So, seeing as you knew him so well, what was his education?"

"He went to school right here in Liberty."

"For how long?"

"Years and years. Just like we all did."

Father was up. "Objection."

"Sustained. Erase the generality. The witness will not present himself as an expert on the educational duration of his fellow citizens."

"I shall rephrase my question. At what grade was your nephew, Thomas Enright, when he left school? You are under oath, Mr. Murphy, so please be accurate. What grade?"

"The fifth. You see, Tom had an illness that . . ."

Gleason said, "Just answer the questions, Marv. Please don't explain them to the court and the jury."

"And what was Mr. Enright's age when he quit school?"

"Sixteen."

The crowd muttered, until the gavel commanded that their manners improve.

"You say he was sixteen."

"No, on second thought, Thomas might have been seventeen."

"Which was it, sir?"

"Seventeen."

"I see," said Miles Harvey. "Now, if my own schooling serves me, and providing that your nephew failed no grades and was promoted each year, he would have graduated from Liberty High School at the proud age of twenty-four."

Judge Gleason glowered at my father. Miles Harvey smiled at the jury, and said, "So much for the formal education of Thomas Enright. But one further question, Mr. Murphy. How was your nephew employed at the time he drew this map?"

"In the restaurant business."

"Oh, then he *owned* an eatery here in town?"

"Well, not exactly. He was gainfully employed at the Silver Dollar Diner."

"In what capacity?"

Marvin scowled, looking up at Judge Gleason. "Do I have to answer that question?"

Judge Gleason sighed. "Please do."

"Well, at first he handled the garbage, and then he was promoted . . . to dishwasher."

We all laughed.

"No more questions, your honor."

Up front, I saw Elmer Sternlock lean over to whisper in my father's ear. Mr. Sternlock wasn't smiling but my father sure was.

"At this time, the defense recalls Sheriff Rake Tatum to the stand, if the court will please permit."

Judge Henry Gleason scratched his head. Looking at my father, he said, "So allowed, if your opponent has no objection. Jesse?"

Father shrugged, and Rake Tatum occupied the witness box.

"Sheriff Tatum," said Miles Harvey, "I'm sure I don't have to remind you that, under the procedure of recall, you are still under oath."

Rake Tatum nodded.

"Are you familiar, Sheriff Tatum, with this map I now hold up?"

"More or less."

"Would you say that, in fact, you are more familiar with the topography of the vast wilderness west of this town, commonly known as Kipp's Mountain?"

"Yes, sir, I am."

"How long have you been a resident of Liberty?"

"Sixty years. I was born here."

"And how long have you been the sheriff?"

"Since the year 1890. Thirty-three years."

"Have you, Sheriff Tatum, spent any time in the area known as Kipp's Mountain?"

"Considerable."

"Have you ever, for reasons of your job or sociability, visited the current home of the defendant, Justice Lion?"

"Yes."

"How many times?"

"Too often to count."

"So then you know exactly where the defendant resides, and you could, with this larger pin I give you, pinpoint his home on the map."

"Near to . . . providing."

"What are your reservations, sir?"

Rake snorted. "Presuming the map itself is correct and follows the lie of the land as I well perceive it."

My father rose. "Objection."

"Sustained," said Gleason. "The witness may be versed in the real estate itself, but is not established as a professional critic as to the drawing of maps."

"But you *do,* sir, know where Mr. Lion now holds residence, and so I ask you to place a second pin."

"The map's wrong," Rake said.

"Objection!" My father near to roared.

"Sustained. Rake, do your best. Enough of us in town have gotten ourselves lost up there. Happens every year in deer season. Been lost up there myself, in a morning fog that was so thick that I couldn't have found my butt with both hands. So just jab in your pin wherever you guess is the right spot."

"I can't."

"Sheriff," said Judge Gleason, "I implore you to comply with the question. And I beg your indulgence as to your personal opinions regarding the map's authenticity."

"Won't do it, Henry."

Elmer Sternlock jumped to his feet. "He damn well better do it, if he wants to keep a badge on his chest."

Henry Gleason pounded harder than ever before. Five times. "Mr. Sternlock! You are out of order, sir. Dare you threaten any officer of this court, or any citizen of this community while in my court-

room, I shall fine you one hundred dollars for contempt. Is . . .
that . . . clear?"

"Sorry, your honor. But that . . ."

"No buts. Our federal government has no jurisdiction in this, or
any, county court. Especially not in *my* court. If you erupt even *one*
more time, you shall not only pay a fine, but you will be barred
as a welcomed observer."

Mr. Sternlock's face darkened to scarlet, as he growled something to my father, who sat at his side. Both of them sat behind a
small table. From the angle allowed me, I could see only part of
Father's face. He didn't look mad at all.

"Darn it," said Judge Gleason, "those doors back there blew
shut. Open 'em up, somebody. Use those two bricks out on the
front porch. Good. Thank you."

Everybody was muttering about the heat, and the many fans were
busy cooling damp faces. Judge Gleason even fanned himself a lick
or two with his yellow legal pad. Then he spoke.

"Where were we?"

Miles Harvey held up the map.

"Sheriff," said the judge, "you and I have lived in this town for
some time. So many years that I'd near blush to add 'em all up."

Rake Tatum nodded.

"However, it would be helpful to the court if you would please
recant, and pinpoint, as defense counsel has requested, the rough
location of Mr. Lion's home."

"I don't know where it is, your honor. On foot, yes. Or rather to
say, on horseback. But I am under oath."

"So you are," said Gleason.

"To be wrong could force me to perjure myself, possible, and so I
now refuse."

"You have no right to refuse, Rake. You know that as well as I
do," Gleason said.

"Beg pardon, but I do have the right to refuse to answer."

"On what grounds?"

"The Constitution of the United States of America. Bill of Rights, if my memory hasn't failed. It's in the Fifth Amendment."

Henry Gleason paused, gavel up, as if about to pound a contempt, or whatever it was called, at Sheriff Tatum. Taking out a white handkerchief from his hip pocket, our county jurist rested his gavel in order to wipe his face.

"Rake, you're right."

"I object," said Miles Harvey.

"Overruled. Is our young counselor so befuddled that he doesn't even know that he's won his point? Excuse me, Mr. Harvey, but the court's shirt is soaked clear through. I think I can speak for everyone in this infernal building, that must have been designed in ventilation by local mapmakers and painted by a jackass, that we're all hotter than the hinges of Hell."

The audience loved it. Both camps seemed to appreciate Henry Gleason's summation of the weather. My own behind was either dead or asleep, as the folding chair I sat on was about as much fun as a permanent cramp. I felt like a boiled potato.

Henry Gleason pounded his gavel.

"I declare this trial, People versus Lion, to be in recess until ten o'clock tomorrow morning."

For all of us, it was school let out.

Sitting in the rear of the courtroom put me close to the door so I was the first one to explode from the courthouse and its August heat. Everyone in town was commenting on how hot it was. "Hotter," somebody cracked, "than Henry Gleason's red suspenders."

I looked across the room and I saw Blessing.

Between her and Hem was Dolly Lion, their mother. Her face was pale, as if the joy of life had been roasted out of her. Hem and Dolly noticed when Blessing took note of me. There was a hard look in Hem Lion's eye. Yet he didn't stop his sister.

Blessing came to me. I wanted to take her in both arms and hold her hard, and long. But we didn't touch. All we did was look at each other's face. Then, pulling a clean white linen from her hand-basket, she gently reached over to blot the wet from my face. Under my eyes. Even though the cloth was now damp, and limp, she held it to her lips.

"Muncie," she said softly, "you stick by your pa, you hear? While I abide to mine. You don't have to become no Lion for my heart. All's you're to be is a Bolt."

"It's all so rotten sad, isn't it."

Blessing nodded. "But there's no night that don't lighten up. So I suspect it'll dawn."

"I hope so."

"Then you'll stand to your lawyer pa?"

"I'll stand. Because I know that Father's like Rake Tatum, in a way. His job is his job. There's bitter in it. Sometimes more than sweet."

Blessing said, "I best go. Ma need me close by her. And to Hem."

"Someday," I told her. "When the better times come . . ."

"We belong, Muncie. You and me."

I smiled at her. "We belong, Blessing."

Chapter 18 ✒

"More beans?"

My father stood at our kitchen stove, holding the handle of the stewpan and a big spoon.

"How many are left?" I asked.

"Only a few. What say you eat half and I'll eat the rest? Can't afford to waste food."

"Pile it on."

We ate. Boiled beans, potatoes, about three frankfurters apiece, along with a can of Boston brown bread. For dessert, we cleaned the icebox out of the last two helpings of strawberry ice cream. And topped off by a glass of milk.

"Boy, that was a nifty supper," I said.

"Good to be home?"

I nodded. "How did it go today?"

"You were there."

"Sure was."

"I noticed you had changed your seat in the audience. Any particular reason?"

"Well, I got to thinking a bit."

"That's always useful."

"So I figured maybe in the morning I'd sit on the Lion side, and come afternoon, I would take a seat behind the prosecution. Behind you."

"Ah," said Father, "the sweet balance of reason."

"I got to thinking on what you told me, the other day, about how to disagree without being disagreeable."

"And you concluded . . ."

"You and Henry Gleason have disagreed in court for years. Case after case."

"Indeed we have. Henry and I have never quite made up our minds as to whether we're friends, or enemies."

"It'd be my guess you're friends and neither one of you know it yet."

Father wiped the milk from his mouth with a napkin. "As surprised as I am to admit, I could have darn near jumped up on the bench this afternoon, and hugged old Henry."

"When he yelled at Elmer Sternlock."

"Right. And also when he so graciously backed off from what could have been a bloody confrontation with Rake Tatum."

"Do you think Judge Gleason's doing a good job?"

"Quite. Oh, I'll admit that when Henry was appointed county judge, I had a few dark misgivings."

"I bet."

"But I'll give this to Henry, he has really grown into his robe, despite the fact that Horace Rudder's robe is about three sizes too long. And too hot."

"Is it tough to be a good judge?"

"I reckon it must be, seeing as we have so many poor ones. Son, there's plenty of pressure on Henry Gleason concerning this trial. As a county judge, it's his first. Yet he knows judicial procedure like the palm of his own hand. Henry's a cantankerous old coot, but he neighbors the law. More than that, he's aware of the law's purpose."

"Today sure had some funny moments." I chewed the beans slowly.

"Henry's enjoying himself. And best of all, he showed the people of this county that a judge can often be a human being."

"Like removing his robe."

"But that, Muncie, is only the packaging. Just the outside black wrapper for the taxpayers to see. Even without the robe, in a shirt with no collar, Henry, in his red suspenders, is a real and honest-to-goodness jurist."

"Wow, I never thought I'd hear you pump up Henry Gleason so much."

"Never thought I would. But when he bared his fangs today, Sternlock and his boys knew that Henry wasn't to be taken lightly. It is Henry's courtroom and *nobody* is going to bully him."

"I wanted to stand up and cheer."

"Son, so did I."

"That wouldn't be proper for a D.A."

Father faked a frown. "Not hardly."

"Were you sort of surprised when Mr. Tatum stood his ground, and refused to answer, and even told Judge Gleason so?"

"No, I wasn't surprised. Rake's a sober gent, but there's a lot of Vermont inside our sheriff, plenty of substance that won't be cornered."

"Was it true, about the Fifth Amendment?"

"*That* was some shocker. And it even set old Henry back on his heels. We were all a bit dismayed, we three *learned* attorneys, when Rake introduced the Bill of Rights."

"I wasn't too sure about all that."

"Simple. The Fifth Amendment guarantees that no person has to testify and incriminate himself. Burden to prove guilt rests with the prosecution."

"Sounds like a good law."

"The best. Today, in a way, that particular point went against me. Yet I uphold the principle. And, you noticed, so does Henry."

"Sternlock sounded mean today, when he tried to force Mr. Tatum to answer that question."

"Elmer's a tough gent. A bull ape when it comes to the law. I would call our friend Sternlock a one-dimensional man. Perhaps not to his face, as he's about double my size."

"You're no coward," I said.

"Glad you think I'm not."

"If you want my opinion, prosecuting Justice Lion takes more courage than a lot of men would have."

"Am I brave, or foolhardy?"

"Brave."

"Ha!"

"What's so funny?"

"That's so typical of a child's mind. Take no offense, Muncie, but hear me out. Young people are so one-way, so very rigid in their near-blind certainty of what is right, or wrong."

"Lots of older folks are, too."

"Yes!" Father pointed a lean finger at my face. "You bet they are. Plenty of Liberty people in that courtroom are seeing only one side of the issue."

"I suppose so."

"Sitting, if you will, on *one* side of the room. Your being on *both* sides pleases me far more than if you were rooting only for me, and deaf to the pleas of defense. It is through your eyes, son, that I begin to see what Judge Gleason has to weigh. Both sides."

"You're one heck of a fair guy."

"Perhaps . . . and maybe that's the only paltry reason that I deserve to have sired a fair son."

"You're on both sides, too. I *know* you are. Even if you're the D.A. and all, you still want to present your case and yet have Justice Lion get out of it."

"I want to win. And, by the way, earlier I could have throttled Henry Gleason for appointing young Mr. Harvey to defend."

"But he sounds pretty good."

"Indeed he *does!* Miles Harvey, once he gets his new shoes a bit muddy, is going to be a crackerjack lawyer. I even caught myself rooting for him until I remembered that he's my opponent."

"I bet I know something," I said.

"Tell me."

"You'd like to see Judge Rudder up on the bench, have Henry Gleason prosecuting, and *yourself* defending Justice Lion."

Father smiled. "Bullseye."

"Then I'm right."

"As rain. Oh, what a fine attorney you'd make." Father held up his hands, as if in surrender. "I'm sorry. Won't commit that error again. You'll be a noble preacher, Muncie. The very finest."

"Thanks. You know, what I really want to do, when I get ordained, is to be a minister the way you practice law."

"Very flattering. I hope you do better."

"I want to reach up to God with one hand, and also reach for the people."

"But if you somehow, hypothetically, had to make a choice, Muncie . . ."

"Where would I decide to only reach? That's easy," I said.

"I'd like to know."

"I'd reach to the people. I guess because God is already reaching to me."

Father gently smiled.

"Hey, what are you looking at?" I asked him, because he was just staring into my eyes.

"Your mother."

"We haven't talked about Mother for awhile, have we? Sometimes I don't bring up the subject of her death because I want you to think about other things. And be happy." I looked down at the dishes that I had seen her handle, so many times, in our kitchen.

"Odd, but what you just said, son, about wanting to spare me the pain . . . that is often why I avoid talking about her, to spare you."

I said, "Maybe we just ought to do it, seeing as we both miss her so much. Remember her out loud, to each other, as much as we can."

"And keep her memory fresh."

"I want to talk about Mother right now."

"So do I, as you so often remind me of Laura. Very often. Every time I look at you, or hear your voice, even though your voice is thickening into manhood."

"What did her voice sound like to you?"

"My wife's voice was a flute, mellow and ripe and so very rich with all the promise that we had together. So often, after her passing, I'd look up in the sky and say . . . Lord, you didn't make me strong enough. I am too brittle for such heartache."

"That's sort of strange," I said.

"What is?"

"I look up in the sky, too. Remember what you said about seeing her whenever you look at my face?"

"Yes."

"With me, I see my mother in the sky, in the soft blue or pink, mostly in the evening when the day's about to die."

"I'm glad we're talking, Muncie."

"Me too."

"We lawyers talk so much, especially when we are lecturing on conduct to our sons, saying so many uppity words that the real words, from inside, somehow miss getting spoken."

"From now on," I said, "we'll get them said."

"We shall." Father looked at the kitchen window that was over the sink. "Sometimes, even now, when I'm working out in the back yard, I can look to the window and see her, waving to me."

I wanted to say something. But I waited, knowing that he was seeing Mother. And I saw her, too. Compared to my father, I didn't have near as much to remember, and for this I felt sort of cheated. Yet glad in a way. Thankful that my father had so many more memories, too personal to let anyone in on.

It made me think of Blessing.

My heart beat more strongly, and I tried to sit still, a habit that Father often told me that I should form. To be master of my motions.

Then I thought about Mrs. Bly and all her family. How she'd moved the mare into a pool of shade, near the courthouse. How I wanted to say "Mother" to somebody. But instead, I'd just try real hard to be grateful that I lived with a man that I enjoyed saying "Father" to.

I said it. "Father."

"Yes?"

"Shucks, it's so dumb I can't even explain, but I just wanted to say it. That's all."

"That's plenty reason enough, son."

"I'm sorry about that note that I wrote to you, before I ran off."

"Well, it's over. Isn't it?"

"I'll stick around."

"Just think how you'd feel if you couldn't attend the trial. Somehow, I knew you'd be there. Cocksure."

"I hid this morning. In back."

"But I *felt* you, Muncie. Before I saw you."

"Honest?"

Father nodded. "Yes, a very positive feeling, strong and clean as a spirit. Not that you're an angel. Yet your soul was in that court-room. I know, I'm sounding like a spook."

"We both have souls, I guess."

"Let's hope so. Golly, it's hard to preach to one's son, about what's right and wrong. And if I ever do, please remind me that if all the ancient philosophers were baffled over the morality issue, then how come old Jesse Bolt knows so much."

"You're not old."

"No? I feel like a hundred. Today was a rugged day in court."

"Will tomorrow be any easier?"

"Worse."

"How come?"

"Because tomorrow, I may have to face a task that I shall surely not enjoy. I dread it like a dog."

"What's it going to be?"

"Tomorrow, I fear that our young Mr. Harvey is going to put the defendant on the stand."

"He doesn't have to."

"No, of course not."

"I bet *you* would if you were defending."

"Yes and no. On the yes side, I'd be confident that Justice Lion, even in his homemade clothes, is an imposing figure. Those eagle eyes and that barrel chest apologize to no one. And just about any juryman I know would look at Justice like he's Jehovah."

"Tell me the no side."

Father came over to sit with me, at our table. "Okay, let's suppose for the moment that I'm defending, and Henry Gleason is prosecuting. Now then, I decide to put my client in the witness chair."

"I bet I know why you'd be worried."

"Very well. Why?" asked Father.

"Because, even though Uncle Justice would be impressive, on his own behalf, you'd have to let Henry Gleason cross-examine."

"Right. Strong as he is, old Justice, a courtroom is *not* his home ground. It is Henry's. And I can see a horrible scene. Henry Gleason, that little rooster, would peck big old Justice to bits, and eat him raw."

"I guess I know your problem."

"Do you?"

"Sure. Tomorrow, you have to cross-examine, and peck away at Justice. Make him look to the jury as a liar and a crook, and a criminal who belongs in prison, because he broke the law."

"That's my duty."

"You know, I'm sitting here trying not to hate *you*. Just hate your job."

"My boy, no one could loathe my job more than I do. And to think that it's what I have so hungered for, years and years. What a fool is man."

"You're no fool."

"Perhaps not. Yet wiser now than a few days ago. Here I be, the county prosecutor, just what I always dreamed. And it's one hairy nightmare."

I laughed. "You wanted it."

Father chuckled. "So I did. And I laugh because I don't know what else to do."

"You'll weather it."

"Lord, I hope so. I could kick Justice Lion for stilling whiskey, boot his big arse so hard that his nose would bleed. For getting caught. And I could kick myself, Henry Gleason, Elmer Sternlock, and even Rake Tatum's pig."

Both of us were shaking. It had been some time since my father had to take off his glasses to wipe the mirth from his eyes. He did it now.

"I could kick you, too," I said.

"Then do it. Maybe they ought to pass a law up in Montpelier."

"Like what?"

"A statute requiring that all lawyers in the state bend over once a week and get a healthy boot on the butt from every foot in town."

Again, I had to hang onto the table, because my sides were hurting a bit. When I thought of what I'd say next, I could just barely get it out:

"How about Marv Murphy's nephew?"

"He'll be next. For a minute today, in court, I thought Henry Gleason was going to jump up, run down the aisle to down the hall, and kick open Marv's safe."

"Stop." My arms were around my aching belly. "I can't take any more."

Father was chuckling. "Today wasn't a trial. It was a freak show. Henry up there yelling in his red suspenders, swearing at the windows, and at his wife's brother. Tomorrow, he'll probably appear in spangles and pink tights."

"Please," I begged. "I can't take it."

"Neither can I. But let's milk it all, son. Every drop. It may be our last laugh." His face drained, and he was again the quiet and sober lawyer, Jesse Bolt.

He was again the district attorney.

Chapter 19 ❧

The next morning the windows had been pried open with a crowbar, and our courtroom was cooler.

"The People versus Justice Lion," intoned Rake Tatum through his nose.

Judge Henry Gleason cleared his throat. "Does the prosecution wish to call further witness at this time?"

Father stood. "No, your honor."

"Defense will proceed."

"Your honor," said Miles Harvey, "I will now ask my client to take the stand in his own defense." As the audience muttered, Justice walked forward, and was sworn in by Sheriff Tatum. He wore his black suit, a clean shirt, and some white stockings inside his old shoes. Yet he could have been a Roman senator.

"Please state your name," said Mr. Harvey.

"I am Justice Lion." As he spoke, the courtroom stilled to hear his every word.

'Sir, where do you reside?"

"Uproad, on my own property."

"Mr. Lion, could you please help the court and the jury by telling us exactly where?"

"Kipp's Mountain."

"Do you rent this real estate from anyone, sir, or do you have a deed?"

"Neither one. To my forefather, Kipp Lion, our land was granted by King George of England."

The crowd mumbled.

"Our right to the land dates back to before the Revolution, and before the Indian War. Earlier than statehood. We wasn't even no colony. Nobody here but red Indians and a few Frenchies."

"Please tell the jury how this parcel of land was called when your family first settled here."

"Verdmont. In French, it's green mountain."

"Sir, was this property a part of any larger grant?"

"At the original, it was a west section of what later got known as New Hampshire. They claimed it, just like all them Yorkers from crosslake."

"And did your forebearers, Mr. Lion, pay taxes to either New Hampshire or New York collectors?"

"Not a red cent."

Everyone, on both sides of the aisle, voiced their approval of Vermont independence, especially in the matters of tribute. Judge Gleason had to gavel our return to silence.

"But you and your family pay taxes now."

Father stood. "Objection."

"Sustained," grunted Gleason. "Counsel will rephrase the question, *and* in the future, choose his wording in a more lawyerlike manner."

"Sorry, your honor. I shall reword my question, Mr. Lion. Do you pay taxes now?"

Justice scowled. "Yes, and I always have, since my father, Sterling Lion, died."

"How much do you pay?"

"Fourteen dollar a year. My brothers all pay, too. As to how we feel about it, all I can say is, they best not ask for one penny more."

The crowd applauded.

"Order," warned the judge.

"Are you married, Mr. Lion?"

"Yes."

"With children?"

"I got twenty. Some's grown and flew off to faraway shores. Two are left, a son and a daughter, and they live to home with me and the woman."

"And, as head of your household, do you support your family?"

"Ain't that a man's mission?"

Judge Gleason said, "The witness will answer."

"Yes, I put bread on our table. Sometimes what we eat ain't all that fancy, but we bow our thanks for it."

"Amen," a few whispered.

"Mr. Lion, if the jury, by some stretch of imagination, finds you guilty of charges, and you are fined and imprisoned, who could feed your family?"

Hem Lion stood up from his seat. "I will."

"Order! No visitor in this courtroom, regardless of how lofty his purpose, will offer comments into the proceedings of this trial. Please be seated, young man," said Judge Gleason, "or else I shall instruct Sheriff Tatum to escort you from the hall. Witness will answer the question."

"We'll make do."

"Mr. Lion, were you arrested on the twentieth day of August of this year?"

"I was."

"And, at the time of the apprehension, was a writ of search presented to you by either Sheriff Tatum or by Mr. Elmer Sternlock?"

"No."

"At such time, were you at work on state land, or on township land . . . or were you standing on your own property?"

"Like usual, I was on Lion land."

"You're sure?"

"Dead right I am. And it be our land for miles in all directions."

"Can you furnish proof of such a statement?"

"I can."

Reaching a big hand inside the bulk of his shirt, Justice Lion withdrew a modest-sized roll of deerskin. To me, it looked little bigger than a rolled up table napkin.

"What I now unfurl," boomed Justice's bass voice, "is our land grant. Near to two hundred year old."

"If I may interrupt," said Gleason, "it would please this court and jury, plus the assembly, if the defendant would read aloud his title."

"I cannot."

Gleason squinted. "You mean because the print is too small, or too old, or what?"

"I don't know how to read."

The judged coughed. "That being the case, would the defendant permit *my* reading the title aloud?"

"No. My son, Hemming, will read it, as he is my heir and my pride. I now ask Hemming to read this grant because his time is come to know its meaning and its worth."

Judge Gleason looked at my father. "Jesse, is that agreeable to you as well as to defense counsel?"

Father nodded. "I so agree."

"Well I *don't.*"

Obviously annoyed, Gleason turned his head to glare at Elmer Sternlock. "May I remind all present that the court, and *no one else,* shall determine legal procedure. Also, the court needs no instruction in jurisprudence. Perhaps our visitors from Washington are accustomed to more formality. Therefore, I shall remind them that the County Court of Addison in Vermont State is not a procedural jurisdiction, but rather a substantive one."

"But your honor . . ."

"Our purpose here, Mr. Sternlock, is to unearth the *facts* of the case. And the relative veracity of fact will be determined neither by the court nor law enforcement officials, but by our local jury. Of which, may I add, *you* are not a member. So I'll thank you to keep mum."

Sternlock's face was red as he sat down.

"I am too old a man, Mr. Sternlock, to be impressed or intimidated by neighbors, or strangers. This bench and its peeling varnish, humble though it may appear, is mine to manage. This trial shall be no podium for any visitor to employ, in order to instruct the court in urbane sophistication."

Sternlock scowled.

"In short, sir," Henry Gleason continued, "keep your dang nose out of the court's business, and your rear end on your chair."

To my ears, it sounded as if all Vermont was applauding. I clapped until my hands hurt and I was the last one, along with Mrs. Bly, to quit.

Henry Gleason wasn't quite through. "If, by any chance, there is an appeal, and People versus Lion climbs to a higher court, and our findings are reviewed, it won't be the first or last time that I fall victim to reverse."

Elmer Sternlock said nothing.

Henry Gleason sighed. Wiping his glasses, he returned them to a face that looked more flushed than usual. "Now then, the court requests that Mr. Hemming Lion step forward, and read aloud this document."

Hem looked taller. As his father handed him the scroll, Hem took it, his back to the bench. Slowly, and with labor, he read:

"Know ye all, in this year of 1731, the Crown of England do hereby bequeath and bequest a parcel of land in New England, located to the east of the Lake of Champlain. This forest wilderness is found to be in an easterly direction, and slightly north, from a location described by the Mohawk tribe of Iroquois Indians and by the British military, as Ticonderoga, a point of land where George Lake enters the larger body of water, Lake of Champlain. The recipient of such tract is a loyal Britisher subject, by name Kipp Lion, and he shall maintain and colonize such parcel under the protection of God and the Crown. The mountain is bounded by Lake Champlain valley land to the west, another valley eastward, and two dry creeks that abut north and south. This land shall ever be entrusted to Lion and his heirs by the Throne of England, thus do I now add signature with wax and seal. George Rex."

The courtroom was dead silent as Justice Lion looked at his son, smiling. "Thank you, boy." He took back his paper. "I know you seen it before. But this time's as honest as any to hear yourself read it straight out."

No one seemed able to speak. We just sat like statues, watching Justice Lion look at Hem, as if the trial mattered so little. And the Lion land mattered so much.

"Thank you, son," said Henry Gleason in a somewhat hoarse voice. "I believe I can speak for every Vermonter in this room when I say that we have just heard a hunk of history that belongs to all of us. Not the land. But surely the words of an English king. And you have read your title in a Lion's voice, befitting a treasured heritage of our community, our state, our nation and all her people."

"Hear, hear," said Mrs. Bly.

Mr. Miles Harvey rose to his feet. "Your honor, I have no more questions."

"Cross-examine," said Judge Gleason.

Here it comes, I thought, watching my father stand up to approach Justice Lion in the witness box. Father looked like a mouse before a panther, compared to Justice. I saw him draw in a deep breath before asking his first question.

"Mr. Lion, I now ask you if you have ever heard of a woman, now residing in Rutland town, by the name of Miss Marybell Cook?"

"No, I have not."

"I believe you, sir. However, this woman is twenty-two years old. A year ago, Miss Cook was about to be married, but the wedding never took place. Seems her future groom changed his mind. Do you know why, sir?"

Justice shook his head. "I do not."

"Miss Marybell Cook, a year or so ago, attended a party, given in her honor. And while at that party, she drank some corn whiskey."

"Plenty of people do," said Justice.

Father said, "Miss Cook is now blind."

The audience reacted in a chorus of "ohs."

"Twenty-two years old, and *blind* for the rest of her life. If it please the court, I shall now open this folder to show you, the court, and members of the jury, her photograph."

As the jury passed the picture of Miss Cook from hand to hand, my father continued. "A very pretty young lady, in my opinion. I happen to know her parents, Mr. and Mrs. James T. Cook, and they are heartsick. I have here a deposition, written and signed by both James Cook and his wife, stating the fine health that their daughter formerly enjoyed. Also, I have here a deposition from her physician, Doctor Charles Kemp of Rutland, stating his professional opinion as to the cause of Miss Cook's sudden blindness."

"Objection, your honor. Prosecution has no proof that the beverage consumed by Miss Cook was manufactured by the defendant."

"Jesse," said Henry Gleason, "if you have a connection to make, then best you haul off and do so. The objection is, *for the moment,* overruled."

"Yes, your honor, I have a connection."

"Best you make it into a question for the witness or I'll take steps. Proceed."

"Mr. Lion, now that you are under oath, can you swear by all Holy that you did not run off the corn whiskey that turned Marybell Cook blind?"

Judge Gleason looked at Miles Harvey. "Well?"

"I object, your honor."

"And rightfully so. I am amazed at our district attorney. Is he so unlettered in the law to ask that a defendant prove his innocence? No, Jess. Objection sustained. Burden of proof. And don't try any more of that monkey business."

"Sorry, your honor. I guess I just got to wondering how many Marybell Cooks have lost their eyesight, and will in the future."

"Strike that! Counsel for the people will take a fresh tack, and I again warn you, Jesse. Keep straight."

"I apologize, your honor." Father walked over to the copper cooker that lay on the evidence table. "Mr. Lion, is this from your still?"

"I object! The witness has no obligation to answer that question and incriminate himself."

"Overruled." Judge Gleason smirked. "Counsel for defense should have thought that over before pushing his client into a witness box surrounded by hot copper."

"Yes, it is my still. But I never drawed off no bad whiskey. . . ."

Gleason snapped, "The witness will limit his remarks to the question and *only* that. The quality of your merchandise, Mr. Lion, is not on trial here. The jury will disregard all testimony and all questions from counsel concerning the whiskey made by the defendant as probable cause of blindness."

"Mr. Lion," said my father, "no one is accusing you of inflicting injury to someone's health. So I now ask you, sir . . . for what purpose did you use this copper cooker?"

"I drawed whiskey, Jesse. And you all blessed well know it, so what's the use of this tomfool circus?"

The gallery rumbled. Justice removed his coat. I could see how uncomfortable he was, as he knotted his hands.

"Order. I'll clear you all out of here," said Gleason, "unless you remain mute. Now, may I remind the defendant that he has pleaded innocent to the charge. At least, so was the plea of your attorney. In light of what has just been admitted, Mr. Harvey, do you now solicit a change of plea, from innocent to guilty?"

"No, your honor," said Harvey.

"That being the case," Judge Gleason said, "it is the court's duty to warn the witness that he is under no obligation to profess his guilt. That is the jury's job, Mr. Lion, and neither yours nor mine."

Justice nodded.

Chapter 20 ❧

Proceed."

"If it please the court," my father said, "I will now request that the defendant roll up the sleeves of his shirt."

Miles Harvey objected.

"Overruled, providing that the prosecution can draw a direct association between the charges and the defendant's exposure."

"I can and will, your honor."

Using one big hand and then the other, Justice Lion turned up the worn cuffs of his faded shirt, resting fists in his lap.

Father continued. "Mr. Lion, will you please raise your arms and show them to the jury?"

All eyes seemed to be leaning forward. Even from the rear of the room, I saw the shiny patches on Justice's arms, the burns and scars where the hair no longer grew.

"Mr. Lion," said Father, "I now ask you to tell the jury how you happened to acquire the burns on your forearms."

"You all know," said Justice.

Gleason said, "Defendant will answer."

"From heat."

Father then said, "I believe it to be common knowledge that the copper cooker on a still gets very hot whenever the manufacture of whiskey is in process." He touched the copper cooker, pulling away his hand, as if burned.

"Is that a question, Jess?" asked the judge.

"Your honor, I shall pose one. Mr. Lion, are the scars you bear from making corn whiskey . . . yes or no?"

Justice Lion stood. Slowly he unfastened the buttons of his shirt-front, removing much of his shirt. His chest was a thicket of white hair, broken by a wide slashing scar of silver, running from his left shoulder to just above his belt buckle. The audience gasped. A few of the white-ribbon ladies turned away their faces.

Jerking a thick thumb at his own naked chest, Justice turned to the jury, pointing at one of its front-row members. He spoke in a deep voice:

"Jack Shacklefort, I ask *you* a question. How did I come by this mark on my body?"

We all held our breath.

I knew which juryman was Mr. Shacklefort, as he was a local farmer who had been in our home, in the office to see Father.

Justice said, "I will answer for you. It was when your barn was burning. Me and my brother, Amos, was first to hasten to your need."

"That's the truth, Justice," said Jack Shacklefort. "And there are men in this room . . . and some womenfolk, too, that remember."

Mr. Shacklefort didn't say "thank you," but his eyes said it, straight at Justice Lion. I didn't think he was going to say more, but I was wrong.

"Hank, our youngest boy, was sleeping out to the barn, to nurse his calf that was grieved. Our son is still alive, thank the good God, because of . . . well, I guess some of you recall what Justice done."

A woman stood. "That's a Gospel truth."

"That's Jack's wife," somebody whispered.

Henry Gleason cleared his throat. "Mr. Lion, you may put your shirt back on, please. Enough latitude. Prosecution will proceed."

"The prosecution objects," said Father.

"Sustained. The jury will ignore all discussion of the burning of Mr. Shacklefort's barn, as it is not relevant to the facts of the trial."

Mrs. Bly was up and on her feet. "Well, it's too damn bad, if you ask me, when a . . ."

"Order."

"Ha! Order, my rump. Henry," said Mrs. Bly, "that could've been *your* boy, or one of *mine,* in Jack's barn."

The gallery agreed, mumbling to their neighbors that Petunia Bly was shouting up a valid point. Judge Gleason, however, was not in agreement.

"Mrs. Bly," rasped Henry Gleason, "this court of law does not convene to entertain comments, no matter how well meant, concerning any sentiments that are foreign to the facts of the case at hand. The court realizes that Liberty is a small town, and all of us here have known one another since childhood. Nonetheless . . ."

"You bet we have," said Mrs. Bly, still standing.

"Nonetheless, my dear Petunia," said Gleason, "if anyone in the gallery is allowed to speak out whenever the spirit prompts, we won't give Mr. Lion an opportunity to defend himself."

Petunia Bly sat herself down.

"If," said Henry Gleason, "this is to remain a court of law, we must endeavor to maintain a modicum of decorum . . . *order* . . . and resist turning this trial into either a Chinese firedrill or a Keystone flicker."

"May I proceed?" asked Father.

"Please do."

Mr. Shacklefort rose from his chair in the jury box.

"Now what?" snapped Henry Gleason.

"Your honor, I wish to be excused."

"Why?"

"Well, maybe it won't be fair, that's all. You know, about my barn burning down and all, and how I feel about . . ."

"Sit down, Jack," ordered Gleason. "Please."

We all waited, watching Henry Gleason wipe his glasses, seeming to be in no particular rush. As though to practice the gesture, he gently rapped a few times with his gavel, and then spoke slowly.

"Personally," said Gleason, "there is not one man or one woman in this courtroom who does not have a few mixed feelings concerning this trial, the officers of this court, and the defendant."

Mr. Bly nodded.

"The court realizes that our community would be an unfortunate place to reside, for all of us, were it not for a certain loyalty that we have for our lifelong neighbors. We, the court and the jury, appear before you not as Gods. But merely men. Your fellow citizens who must . . . I repeat, *must* . . . do our duty."

Gleason sighed.

"If I so decide, because of interference from any camp, to declare a mistrial, then what happens? Well, I know a speck or two about the law, so I'll tell you. A mistrial means that the defendant, Justice Lion, will again face a trial in another court. And the state may step in. On this bench, perhaps in this very room, you will inherit another trial judge. He may be better, or worse."

The audience mumbled.

"And, you'll have another jury. Perhaps strangers. Folks who don't give a blast of backside mule gas about this town of Liberty, or what happens to anyone who is proud to say . . . I live here, and this community is my home."

We all sat more quietly.

"This trial, People versus Lion, is a sorry business. So far, it's been one merry Hell of a mess. Yet, it is *our* mess. Therefore, if there is one wisp of conscience remaining within us, I believe it is *we* who must clean it up. See it through. Not a very enticing job, is it? But it's *our* job. Yours out there and mine up here."

Henry Gleason rose from behind the bench, stepping carefully down the bare wooden stairs, to reach the floor of the courtroom.

"I can't promise anyone that the outcome of this trial shall be painless. It won't be. Because courts of law seldom are. I know it's hot in this room. Overcrowded, and not enough chairs for every cheek."

Gleason smiled.

"Let me remind you all of one fact. As an attorney, and as a prosecutor, I have logged many an hour, many a day, and may I add, many a decade in this old pelter of a building. And I oozed out more buckets of sweat here than you have. This pesky edifice is our county courthouse, yours and mine."

Judge Gleason removed his glasses.

"I have laughed in this room, more than once, usually when Horace Rudder, God rest him, was looking up the law. And, my friends, I have also wept."

He turned to my father.

"So has Jesse. We've had some hairy times and happy times here, haven't we, Jess?"

Father slowly nodded.

"Help me," said Henry Gleason. "I beg all of you to let us spit on our hands and have at it. Do so, and you will be proud of yourselves, and the white spires of Liberty, our little town, will stand taller in the eyes of all Vermont."

"I'm sorry, Henry."

It was Mrs. Bly who had spoken, in an unusually soft voice. Henry Gleason looked at her and winked an eye.

"Accepted, my lady. Freedom of speech is what we all believe in, Petunia. So long as it doesn't tread on the toes of those whose freedom it is to listen."

Again, the judge turned to my father. "Jesse, you feel like adding anything to my little sermon? Miles? Now that I've come so close to turning myself into a jackass, I don't want to bray alone."

"Your honor," said my father, "I never dreamed I'd say this in public, but Liberty is proud of her son."

We all clapped.

"Dang this watch," snorted Gleason. "Forgot to wind the cussed thing last night. What's the time?"

Somebody said, "It's near noon."

"Good," said Gleason. "I could eat a horse." He pretended to rap his knuckles, like a gavel, to my father's head. "This court is in recess until one o'clock."

People laughed.

As my legs unfolded, it sure felt great to stand up. Half of the crowd was stretching, and the rest were either yawning or rubbing the circulation back into their hips. A lot were smiling, joking, poking one another.

But not Hem.

As he turned, I saw Hemming Lion's face. The happy eyes were gone; and his face was pale, almost sickly. He stood alone, even though he was among the other Lions, talking to no one. Looking, yet seeing neither anyone nor anything. He was no longer the Hem Lion that I knew . For some reason, I felt a fear of him, as though I didn't dare to seek his company. I didn't want him to see me.

Hem's face was tinder dry. To me, had someone in the courtroom struck a match to light a pipe, my closest friend would explode into flame. He was a breathless loft of dry hot hay.

Blessing was with her mother, Dolly, in the center of more than a score of male Lions which formed a ring around the two females. The men did not speak. Yet their deep eyes spoke to one another in some strange and silent language that was spoken only among up-road ferns. In quiet shadows where even the overhead sparrows were still.

The Lions exited from the courtroom, moving differently from the town people. The Lions were slower; sleepy cats, edging away from the crowd like curls of smoke. People gaped at them. But the Lions did not return the stare. All of them had that same mountain-man look. Quiet, but deep. Dark surface water in the bottom of an unknown and untested well.

They weren't like me, or Father. These were men who stilled whiskey, and could stand motionless for half a day, on a deer watch.

I saw them walk to their wagons. In the bins were blankets, tarps, covers of one kind or another for masking secret cargo. Seeing the muzzle of a shotgun, I wondered if it was as primed and loaded as its owner. Stretching out a lean hand, the man nearest the wagon patted the gunstock as if greeting a friend.

I felt wet.

My body seemed near to fever with the sudden chill; I recalled the night of coon hunting with Hem, and how I'd run off and into capture by two of Hem's cousins. Again I felt the blindfold cut my face. And once more my stomach almost burned from swallowing their whiskey. I wanted to run. Yet I stood there in the shadow of a courthouse elm, observing the Lion clan as they quietly watered their horses and mules. They toted handmade wooden buckets from the public pump.

The Lions looked so calm.

Didn't they know that Justice didn't have much of a chance? And yet Hem's reading aloud the land grant from King George might have swayed the jury a bit. It sure was impressive. Almost like acting out a play; the way we did sometimes, in school, for Mrs. Travers.

"Muncie."

Turning around, I saw my father walking toward the elm under which I waited. He was smiling.

"Howdy," I said.

"Quite a morning, eh?"

"Sure was."

Father touched my shoulder, resting his hand as we walked toward home, to eat lunch. His other hand carried his old brown and battered leather briefcase with one broken strap. The thought hit me that my father didn't look as spiffy as his opponent. Miles Harvey was across the street, wearing a light blue suit and a bright silvery tie. His shoes sparkled a fresh shine. Looking down, I saw my father's footwear, which sort of matched his briefcase. All tired out.

"In a way I hope you win," I said.

He looked at me. "Honestly?"

"Sort of the same way I want the court to be lenient, as you say, and maybe just give Uncle Justice a scolding. And send him up-road, back home."

Father smiled. "That would be ideal."

"Not just that. I'd also like to see Mr. Elmer Sternlock blow a gasket. Wouldn't you?"

"If he does, I would surmise that our new jurist, Judge Gleason, will pin his ears back. Perhaps even throw a contempt his way."

"He was nearing doing that to Mrs. Bly," I said, "or so it seemed to me."

Father shook his head. "Not hardly. I know Henry too well. And he, like everyone in town, knows Petunia Bly as a well-intended citizen."

"I liked it," I said, "when Judge Gleason stepped down from behind his big old desk and talked to all of us."

"Did you?"

"Didn't *you,* too?" I asked.

"Have to admit I did. Henry, in his cagy and countrysome way, was rather eloquent. Fact is, I was a bit moved, not so much by his language, but by the simple logic behind it. Even more so by the sentiment that Henry holds in his heart for Liberty."

"I liked what he said a whole lot."

"As did I. Henry's becoming a bit mellower, or a mite more cantankerous, and darn if I know which'll come next."

"He wants to do a good job as judge."

"Indeed he does. Henry tries. The old goat is giving this trial all he's got. He's already a judge, Muncie. And he proved it today. Oh, I warn you, if old Henry gets fired up, he'll call a mistrial. Only, however, as a last resort."

"That's what he threatened to do," I said.

"More like half a threat. All in all, what I admire most about Henry is that he's showing no fear of getting the judgment reversed in an appeal. This is *his* show, *his* ballpark, and he fully intends to ump the game. Call the balls and strikes as he sees them, one by one, as they sizzle over the plate."

"I'm real glad you're a lawyer." As I spoke I punched his arm.

"You are, eh?"

"Sure am. You'd enjoy this trial no matter which side you were on."

Father said, "Enjoy it and hate it. If an attorney is to ever begin to save his soul, I believe he has to have a few mixed feelings. Rarely is an issue one-sided, son."

"I know."

"Bully for you. Our human condition is not a recipe of absolutes. You may have concluded that Elmer Sternlock is an evil character in this drama. Have you?"

"In a way."

"Well, I disagree. Sternlock is a dedicated cop, a mastiff dog, and perhaps no more overzealous than a few preachers and priests in this state. Maybe, if all us hold fast to our reason, we can wade through this old trial with cool heads. And not go raving mad."

I told him, "A lot of us are heated up."

"Quite so. Funny thing, the human rage. It would be my guess, that in the wide range of human emotions, the least helpful is a man's temper."

As he spoke, I thought about Hem Lion.

Chapter 21 ❧

Sheriff Rake Tatum said, "All rise."

As we stood, into the courtroom marched Henry Gleason, once again wearing his black robe. Judge Gleason seated himself up behind the bench and the case of People versus Lion was again underway. He rapped the top of his desk.

"Will the defendant, Justice Lion, please retake the witness box," said Gleason.

Justice Lion stood. "No. I said all that needs saying. I'm all spoke out."

Henry Gleason looked at Father. "Does the prosecution wish to continue a cross-exam of the defendant? If so, Mr. Lion must testify."

"No, your honor."

"Then," said Henry, "the defense may call its next witness."

"Thank you, your honor," said Miles Harvey. "At this time, we call to the stand Mrs. Harry Bly."

Petunia Bly got sworn in by Rake Tatum and then Miles Harvey asked her to state her name.

"Petunia Maxwell Bly."

"How long have you lived in the town of Liberty, Vermont?"

"My whole blessed life. And now you best not ask for that in years, sonny, because a woman's got a right to secret her age. Right?"

Several bonnets nodded in the crowd. And I heard plenty of chuckles from all sides.

"Tell us, Mrs. Bly, whether or not you personally know the defendant, Mr. Justice Lion."

"Course I do. And I dare say I know Justice near better than any of the townsfolk in this room. Or as well."

"In your own words, Mrs. Bly, would you please inform the court and the jury as to the character of the defendant."

Mrs. Bly winked at Justice. "Yup, he's a *character* all right."

Judge Gleason shook a warning finger at Mrs. Bly. "Elaborate, would you please?"

"Well, I just *know* him, that's all. Knew his sister, Miriam, too . . . before the Lord took her."

The crowd mumbled, "Amen."

Petunia Bly sort of half smiled at the audience, a grin that was more from nerves than ribs. She wore her good pink dress, the one with clumps of black-eyed Susans all over it. She sort of reminded me of an enormous flower bed.

Gleason snorted, "Proceed."

"Mrs. Bly," said Miles Harvey, "again I shall ask you to please give us an accounting of the defendant's moral character, as you know it."

Opening her firmly-set lips, Petunia Bly said, "We got ourselves a good town. Liberty's a decent place to bring up . . ."

Gleason's gavel whacked his bench. "Dang it, Petunia, come to the point. This court does not convene to hear testimony concerning either Miriam Lion or the township. Stick to the subject, the defendant."

"Yes, your honor," said Mrs. Bly. "Well, lots of us here today was also present yesterday, when Justice peeled off his shirtfront to expose his scar. And we heard about Jack's barn, not that too many of us ain't remindful. It weren't the first time that the Lions was part of us, even if they choose to live uproad."

"Is that all?" asked Gleason.

"No, not by a durn sight. Must be at least ten years ago when my sister's boy, Hayward, got himself lost up yonder. And it was the Lions that found him and carted him home to safe and sound. We can thank Justice for that, and will, from now to all eternal."

"Are you now, Mrs. Bly," asked Miles Harvey, "telling all of us, including the jury, that in your opinion, Mr. Lion has been a good citizen?"

Father stood. "Objection."

"Sustained. Counsel for defense will not," said Judge Gleason, "put words in the mouth of the witness. Best you rephrase."

"Sorry, your honor. Mrs. Bly, what kind of a citizen and a neighbor has Mr. Lion been?"

"A doggone good one. If you ask me, the people in Liberty are blessed lucky to have Lions in our hills, instead of some of them . . . *tribes* . . . that reside further north, like the Korjacks. I can't abide no thought of Justice Lion in a jail cell. Not him. No man what done as much good in this valley deserves to get put behind bars. And no good Christian would do such."

Mrs. Bly quickly stood up, shaking a stern finger at the jury, and then her fist was punching the empty air. About half of the gallery applauded.

"Order," shouted the judge. "And please do sit down, Petunia, before you blow your boiler. It's plenty hot enough in here without your adding more steam."

Before sitting, Mrs. Bly adjusted a bulge on her hip, which could have been the hem of her corset.

"Your honor," said Miles Harvey, "I believe that, in her own unminced words, Mrs. Bly has testified most adequately as to the defendant's character, and his past contributions to the community. No further questions."

Placing both of her red hands on the front edge of the witness box, Mrs. Bly prepared to pull herself up, hoping to be excused.

"Cross-examine," said Henry Gleason.

Father rose to his feet.

"Mrs. Bly, all of us here were much relieved when your nephew, young Hayward, was finally located up on Kipp's Mountain, and returned to home and hearth."

I saw Mrs. Bly nod.

"However, regardless of your personal esteem for the defendant, was it really *he* who found the lad . . . or was it, if you would please summon your memory to recall, the defandant's *brother,* Amos Lion?"

Mrs. Bly glowered at my father.

"Witness will answer the question," said Gleason.

"Maybe it was the brace of 'em, I don't right remember."

"Oh," said Father, "you don't remember? Well, it so happens that I myself remember, as I was part of the search party that night. And, as I clearly recollect, it was Amos Lion who discovered your nephew." Father glanced up at the bench. "Sorry, your honor. I shall now restate the above in the form of a question, reminding the witness that she is under oath."

Crossing the apron of the courtroom, Father lifted up the black Bible from the long table, holding it so all could clearly see it. "My question, Mrs. Bly, is this. Was it Justice Lion who found your sister's boy, or was it Amos?"

Petunia Bly's hands became big pink fists as she scowled at my father, who still held the Holy Bible high in the air. Then she stared at the book.

"It could have been Amos."

"Thank you, Mrs. Bly," said Father. "We all realize that your nephew got himself lost a good many years back, and I beg the court's indulgence in allowing you to amend your testimony."

As my father paced to and fro in front of the witness box, he continued to carry the Bible in his hand. Mrs. Bly was starting to perspire. Her face was becoming shiny. I noticed how her eyes followed my father, back and forth, staring at the black Bible.

"Mrs. Bly, are you a member of one of our local churches here in Liberty?"

"Yes."

"Good. Which one?"

"The Methodist."

"And do you and your family attend services at the Methodist church with regularity?"

"We go every Sunday."

"Would you consider yourself, Mrs. Bly, one of the more active women in your church's *social* activities, those being apart from the formal services on the Sabbath?"

"I'd say that I try to be."

"How so?"

"Well, for our spring and fall rummage sale, and our youth club, and like that."

"Interesting," said Father. "And, in addition to the aforementioned activity, do you also participate in preparing some of those delicious suppers at the church?"

"Sometimes I help out."

"Ah, so sometimes you help out. Come, come, Mrs. Bly. Aren't you becoming a bit modest? Isn't it a locally-known *fact* that you oversee much of the cooking in the church kitchen, and plan which baked goods will be served?"

"I do my best."

"And, as to the baking of those goodies, who actually does that?"

"We all pitch in . . ."

"Meaning, of course, that you *personally* engage in the preparation of bread, rolls, cupcakes, pie, cake, shortcake, pudding . . ."

"Once in a while."

Father turned to Elmer Sternlock. "Mr. Sternlock, do you have a certain list in your pocket, a list which you showed to me one evening at my home?"

"Yes, I do."

"May I borrow that list, please?"

"Here." Sternlock handed the list to my father.

"This piece of paper I now hold," said Father, "represents the amounts of sugar delivered to the grocers of Liberty by wholesalers. But, I believe it is of little interest to the court and to our jury, as we all know who *sells* sugar here in town. What may interest all of us is the question . . . who *buys* it?"

Reaching into his shirt pocket, my father produced a second slip of white paper, about the size of a small envelope.

"Your honor, I have here information from all three of our local grocers, and on *this* list, the *names* of persons who purchase large amounts of sugar."

Right then, I noticed that Mrs. Bly was busily wiping her steaming face with a hanky. Afterward, she began to fan herself with it.

"I will now show this list of sugar buyers to the witness," Father said, "asking her to read us the name that tops each of the three columns of names."

Mrs. Bly looked at Judge Gleason.

"Witness will comply."

"I don't have my glasses," she said.

"Ha!" snorted Henry Gleason. "Surely the witness can see well enough to read her own name. B-L-Y. Show it to the jury, Jess."

Twelve men leaned forward to examine the list of sugar buyers. Almost to a man, each one read the list, immediately glancing up from the paper to look at the witness.

"So I bake a lot for the church," said Mrs. Bly. "What of it?"

"How often," Father asked, "do you Methodists throw a supper? Every night?"

"No."

"Once a week?"

"No, not that often."

"How often, Mrs. Bly? Isn't it more like six times a year, every other month?"

"Something like that."

"Was there a supper at the Methodist church during the month of June?"

"No, not in June."

"In July then?"

"We don't have suppers in the summer. It's too hot back in that kitchen. We have three in the spring and three in the autumn."

"None in June or July. None at all?"

Mrs. Bly shook her head. "No."

"Nevertheless, Mrs. Bly, do you know how much *sugar* you purchased during the months of June and July?"

"I don't recall." As she spoke, it appeared to me as if she was holding her breath, so that no more lies would be told through her lips.

"Well, I'll tell you, Mrs. Bly. In the two-month period of June and July of this year, you purchased exactly *two hundred pounds.*"

The crowd gasped and whispered. Mrs. Bly was trembling.

Bending low, Father ducked under the long courtroom table in order to yank an object from below. Arms shaking, perhaps more than was necessary, he held a white fifty-pound bag of sugar over his head.

"Gentlemen of the jury, this one bag contains fifty pounds of sugar."

I heard a soft *thud* as my father dumped the fifty-pound bag at the base of the bench, upon a narrow ledge, so that the white sugar bag stood erect. He repeated his theatrics with a second bag, a third, and finally a fourth.

"These four bags, I now inform the court and the jury, weigh exactly two hundred pounds. Allowing that Mr. and Mrs. Bly have a large family, nonetheless, this is one powerful lot of sugar to consume in a period of just sixty days."

Father paused to lick some white grains of sugar from the tips of his fingers. "Surely, I say to our jury, one would require quite a sweet tooth to devour that much sugar."

The jury nodded. Mrs. Bly seemed frozen in her witness chair, as if hogtied by knowing what was going to happen.

"And," my father continued, "a person would be required to earn quite an income to pay all our three local grocers. None of whom, I presume, are well known for passing out free samples of sugar." Father's voice was cold and hard.

Gleason snorted. "Come to the point, Jesse."

"Gladly, your honor." He turned to face Mrs. Bly once again, reaching for the Bible. "I now ask the witness if she, whose hand touched this very Bible and swore by Almighty God to tell the truth, can tell us how she used two hundred pounds of sugar. And how she could afford to purchase such amounts on the wages of a part-time housemaid. Are you a banker, Mrs. Bly?"

Petunia Bly said nothing. Covering her eyes with the white hanky, she hid her face from all of us in the courtroom. It was as if she was praying to die.

"Witness will answer the question," said Gleason, "as to how the sugar she purchased was employed."

I could hear her start to sob.

"No," said Father quietly to the jury, "our witness surely does *not* want Justice Lion to go to jail. For if so, what would befall her sugar-procuring enterprise? How much profit do you make from this nifty little venture, Mrs. Bly?"

"Please . . ." She was almost choking. . . . "Please . . ."

"So much for the character reference," my father said to the jury. "And to the character of illicit whiskey, which has tempted a good Christian woman to become an accessory, and an embarrassment to her family and her church."

My spine froze as I heard the sobs from Mrs. Bly. Her entire body was shaking. And she looked to be so ashamed. And my father looked no better. Never had I seen his face so downcast.

Father said, "No more questions."

Chapter 22 ᑫ✤

Rake Tatum stood up.

With his arm around Petunia Bly, he helped her up from the witness box. The white handkerchief was still held over her face, as if she wanted to hide herself from the eyes of all the town. She looked beaten.

The courtroom was surprisingly quiet as we all watched Rake escort Mrs. Bly down the center aisle, to the rear of the courtroom, and out through the open double doors. As she passed by my seat, I wanted to stretch out my hand, to tell her how sorry I was that Father, so ruthlessly, *had* to challenge her testimony. And to discredit her as a character witness. He was just doing his work. I wanted to tell her how much he shared her hurt.

"Proceed," ordered Gleason.

Mr. Miles Harvey stood. "Your honor, we have no more witnesses to call." His voice sounded a bit unsure.

Henry Gleason looked over at my father. "The prosecution will now present its summary to the jury."

Father stood, walked to the jury box, and faced the dozen men.

"Gentlemen, the testimony in the case of People versus Lion is now over and done. You have heard both sides. You have seen the evidence. As a representative of the people of Addison County, it now becomes my duty, as your district attorney, to total up this evidence and this testimony. So that you, the jury, can weigh the facts."

Father cleared his throat. "Fact one. The defendant, Mr. Justice Lion, was caught for manufacturing illicit whiskey, and thus placed under arrest by Sheriff Tatum."

Right away, I noticed that my father was cautious not to mention the name of Elmer Sternlock, an outsider.

"Here"—my father crossed the courtroom to rest his hand on the copper cooker—"is part of the still that Mr. Lion employed. And here"—he held up a mason jar of white liquid—"is a sample of the defendant's whiskey."

A member of the jury coughed.

"We do not gather in this courtroom to determine whether or not the defendant is, or has been, a good neighbor. That is not at issue. What *you* must decide is this: is the defendant guilty of the crime of stilling illegal spirits? And, according to law, it *is* a crime. We do not convene here to evaluate the fairness of such a law. Only to apply this law to anyone, *anyone* who breaks it."

I heard mutterings from deep in the throats of several of the Lions who sat in the audience.

"Our purpose today," Father continued, "is *not* to evaluate the quality of this beverage, or to impose our own personal morality upon those who imbibe. Some folks drink. Others don't. Home brew, the kind of whiskey in this very mason jar, *can* be dangerous. If distilled improperly it can cause bodily harm, and worse, turn a drinker blind. Alcohol has destroyed families in this town. Innocent children have gone without bread and warm clothing, because certain parents became slaves to a bottle."

A few heads nodded.

"And so a law was passed. Like any law created by imperfect men, this law is perhaps not totally perfect. In some ways, I must now honestly confess to you, I am a mite personally opposed. Like you, I have mixed feelings. Yet, if this law can prevent *one* child in Vermont from going to bed hungry . . . or cold . . . and one beautiful young lady from losing forever her eyesight, then I stand by this law."

"Amen," someone whispered.

"Good men sometimes do foolish things. The Almighty did not create us to be angelic creatures. We all are faulty beings, rife with shortcomings, riddled with characteristics that make us all, at times, contrite. How often we all must bow our heads to beg forgiveness. I wonder, dare we excuse ourselves from the unpleasant duty of protecting the drinker? More than that, offering our protection to the innocent, the dependents who go without food, because of a father's weakness for liquor."

Father cleared his throat. "Some of our fellow citizens here in Liberty wear the white ribbon of Temperance. I do not. Yet I must applaud those who do. Now, returning to the elements of this trial, a law was passed. If this law proves unsound, it may well be voided. Already our ears hear rumblings of repeal. But, as long as this law stays on the books, it is our duty to honor it, obey it, apply it to any citizen and to all citizens who break the law."

The courtroom became very still.

"Our defendant, Mr. Justice Lion, has broken the law. We meet in this room not to judge the *man,* nor to judge the *law.* Only to apply this law to the lawless."

Behind the huge desk, the chair squeaked as Judge Henry Gleason shifted his position, his eyes never leaving my father.

"Yes, gentlemen of the jury, we know what the law demands. Like any legal statute, this law deserves to be honored by all men. Let no man defy it. Let no man claim he alone is above the law, for if we allow that, we erode that which is most precious in our community . . . civility. If our town, our county, our state or nation turns its back to crime, no matter how petty, our society will crumble to ruin."

Father paced back and forth before continuing.

"Each law applies to all mankind. If we ignore this concept, then we shall surely see our dreams decay to the point where every man can break every law."

My hands were starting to sweat.

"Therefore, members of the jury, I ask the twelve of you, based on the evidence seen and testimony heard, to find our defendant, Mr. Justice Lion, *guilty*. Your task is a most unpleasant chore. But far more distasteful is the prospect that could result from your failure to confront such a duty. The faces of Liberty are watching you, awaiting your upholding of this law and all of our law, so that our town shall forever prosper by its own respect."

Father paused. "I ask you to allow our cherished pride that is Liberty to endure."

He sat down.

Gleason spoke. "Defense may address the jury."

I watched Mr. Miles Harvey slowly stand. Spine erect, he walked toward the jury box, looking as fresh as my father appeared wilted.

"Gentlemen," he said, "I am a stranger in your town. A new face. Someone whom you have never known, and have no reason to trust. My opponent, Mr. Jesse Bolt, is a resident here. More than that, he has practiced the law in this county for a long time. Compared to him, I'm little more than a cub in a lion's den."

The jury smiled at his connecting of a family name to his personal situation.

"You see, gentlemen, I'm just a greenhorn. Practically, one might add, fresh out of law school. Guess I'm about the last man on Earth that a man like Justice Lion would ever look to, or need. It was only a few days ago when I met Mr. Lion for the first time."

Miles Harvey smiled. "To tell you men the truth, when I first saw Justice, I was scared to death."

The audience softly laughed.

"What's more, as I learned about this case, and about the man I had been appointed to defend, I grew more afraid every second. Frightened that I wasn't lawyer enough, or seasoned enough, to prevent a man like Justice Lion from rotting in prison."

I watched the audience when Mr. Harvey used the word *prison,* as it seemed to make everyone less than comfortable. No one in Liberty was a jailbird. We sure weren't known for a lot of crime.

"I'd be hard pressed to say how much law I learned in the past week. Maybe not much. But here before you stands one young attorney who has learned a great deal about his client."

Turning around, Harvey looked at Uncle Justice, who returned the glance, unmoved.

"Although it may be foolish to admit such to all of you, I'm a city boy. A man can't help where he's born, can he? In a city, you don't meet families like the Lions. And I say to you now, knowing Justice Lion, for even such a short span of time, has been a rare privilege. He's a man of wisdom, wit, compassion."

Mr. Harvey put his hands into his pockets as he continued to talk.

"Do you know what I expected? I'll tell you. Guess I expected to defend a man who was bitter, sullen, abrim with revenge. Not so. Oh, he was quiet. It took awhile for me to convince him that I was on *his* side. He refused to accept this, at first. Sorry to admit, I did most of the talking, until I finally smartened up to realize that if I was to discover anything at all, best I listen."

As I watched Mr. Harvey, I admitted that he seemed to be off to a good start. Even the judge seemed interested. Henry Gleason sat, motionless and attentive, twisting his eyeglasses with his right hand.

"Knowing my client, as I now know him, I have become . . . enriched. He speaks with fondness about his home, his family, and his mountain. Mr. Lion's concerns are not for himself. Never have I met a human being so at peace with his own soul. And never have I known anyone who knows more about who he is. He is Justice Lion, a man who owns a mountain, a man who *is* a mountain. I behold him far more than just himself. He is Liberty, he is Vermont . . . and he embodies the very spirit of our United States of America."

Harvey pointed at Justice.

"He is freedom. You know, when I was a kid, perhaps in your eyes not too long ago, we used to study our history books and learn about 1776, and how we fought the British and won our independence. Freedom and liberty and independence were always just a pack of uppity words, to me, until this week. Until I became associated, and deeply involved, with this giant of a gentleman from the hills of Vermont. He is a farmer, a woodsman, and a philosopher. Aye, even a poet."

Miles Harvey paused to hold up a single finger to make his next point.

"One book. He told me, that in his cabin up on Kipp's Mountain, there is only one book."

Harvey pointed at the Bible. "This book."

"His daughter, Blessing, who is seated in this courtroom, reads the Bible to her father every evening. Although this man may be intentionally ignorant of the laws of man, he is indeed well versed in the laws of God. To him, Divine law is far more than Biblical chapters. His faith is solid as soil. Looking at him now, I can finally appreciate the feeling that Jesus of Nazareth had for Simon whom He called Peter, the rock."

Miles Harvey sighed.

"That's a lawyer's trick, isn't it? Always quoting the Good Book to win a case. Or free a scoundrel. I apologize. I am no Jesus and Justice Lion no Peter. Yet were I to choose a rock upon which to build one humble little chapel of American independent spirit . . . there, good gentlemen of the jury, sits my rock."

Walking to the table where the Bible rested, Mr. Harvey's hand touched it, gently.

"Sorry, folks. I won't use or misuse this Bible anymore. It has been misused enough in our courtroom, to humiliate and embarrass a woman who loves it. And from what I have learned from many of her neighbors, so often lives by it."

I saw heads turn to stare at my father.

"Never," continued Miles Harvey, "have I met a man, beneath a threatening cloud of a prison sentence, more indulgent with his circumstances, or more forgiving of those who arrested him to confinement. Not once, in all the hours that I spent conferring with my client, have I heard Justice Lion speak ill of even *one* fellow citizen."

Harvey smiled. "Not even about Mr. Sternlock."

Sternlock's face colored. He, no doubt, suddenly felt the eyes of the audience looking his way. His face was meaner than a bulldog, so I thought, as though he wanted to haul off and hit somebody. Real hard.

"Your district attorney," Harvey said, "has asked that we *punish* Mr. Lion. Send him to a penitentiary. Lock him up as if he were a common criminal. Place him behind bars. One year is a long time in a jail cell. A long time for any person to serve. I've seen plenty of prisons from the outside, looking in. For many of us, a cell would be considerable discomfort. But for a man like Justice Lion, a year in prison would be an eternal Hell."

Walking over to his client, Miles Harvey rested his hand on the beefy shoulder.

"For this man, torn from the freedom of his mountain home, jail could amount to some hideous and screaming insanity."

We waited for Mr. Harvey to continue.

"For this big bear of a gentleman, the severity of such a sentence could warp the most forgiving man I have ever met into a hardened heart. Is this what you desire to do? Is this our mission here? Can our purpose to punish be so zealous as to destroy in one man the very qualities which so many people in the town have duly honored? I think not."

Mr. Harvey again walked toward the jury.

"Earlier in this trial, we were shown a photograph of a young lady who was blinded by drinking moonshine whiskey, illegally made. All of us saw her face. And so did my client. Last evening, after our day in court had ended, Justice Lion shared his thoughts with me, telling me something that I was ill prepared to hear. Mr. Lion said that, regardless of his trial's outcome, he never again would distill even one more drop of corn liquor."

The courtroom buzzed. Miles Harvey stood tall and straight, not at all the greenhorn that I had thought him to be. His voice became stronger.

"Also, he instructed me not to mention his vow in court, and by so doing, I no doubt annoy him. Yet I believe his sentiments in this matter warrant being shared. Does this mean that Justice Lion, of all people, shall now sport a white ribbon pinned to his shirt? Perhaps not. But I ask you now, which is more sincere . . . that white flag which a man wears outside his breast, or a fervent promise that he holds within?"

Up on the bench, Henry Gleason took out a bandana and silently wiped his nose.

"Gentlemen of the jury," continued the young lawyer, "what exactly is the purpose of a courtroom? To punish, or to correct? If you agree with me that it is the latter, then I say blessed be the man so fluid as to correct himself. Within us all, there is a spirit that stretches up our hand, in aspiration. Perhaps, when we pray, we say . . . Lord, help make me better than I am."

I heard someone mumble an "Amen."

"A few years ago, as a law student, I never dreamed that I would be entrusted with the defense of such an unforgettable man. I have grown in his shadow. My soul has indeed been nourished by his warmth. Never could I ask Justice Lion to become us, to live as we do. Perhaps my most honest wish for all the people of this village, mostly for myself, is that we endeavor to become more like the man that I defend, admire, and by whose side I do battle."

I couldn't tell who said it. But I heard a woman's voice speak up, from somewhere inside the congregation. All she said was "Bless that boy." Mr. Harvey heard it, too. We all did. Yet there was no cocky look on his face. He just looked like a young man who had been graced by his own hard work. As though he had been truly honored to serve his client. He stood in the light from the courthouse window, looking out, up into the outdoor trees.

Then he turned to the twelve silent men.

"So, gentlemen of the jury, I ask your mercy. Justice Lion would not beg for it. But I do. Oddly enough, there are two names among us. Proper names, and they are Justice and Liberty. One a man, the other his town. I ask you to spare the defendant in this trial. Grant him his freedom. For if the circumstances were reversed, and *he* sat upon a chair in this jury box, I feel certain that my client would forgive his fellow man, as he has already forgiven all of us. When there is so precious little hatred in such a giant of a heart, I implore you to look into your own."

Miles Harvey smiled.

"Keep your Justice with Liberty."

Chapter 23 ❧

H enry Gleason cleared his throat.

"Gentlemen of the jury . . . some of you have been jurors several times in this courtroom of ours, and maybe you know a good deal more, about how a trial should be conducted, than I do."

Some of the men smiled.

"It is with some regret that no *ladies* are among you, but as you all know, a jury is not selected by the court, but rather by the opposing attorneys. I congratulate them both, not only for their forthright summations, but also for choosing twelve good citizens. You all have been patient, as well as attentive, and my respect in this matter extends to you all, our worthy and august dozen."

Gleason removed his glasses to grin at his play on words. He seemed to be amused.

"Compared to *your* job, *mine* is a lead-pipe cinch. All I do is sit up here on the bench, gripe about the ventilation, and try my dog damndest to look important."

People chuckled.

"*Your* job is to hear testimony, in order to determine the *facts* of the case. To decide who is telling the truth apart from those who might stretch the garters of the dear old girl who blindly holds the scales."

The laughter came once again.

"Now, at long last, comes the time for your county judge to start earning his salary, paltry though it may be. It is my duty to decide what the *law* is in this case. So that you, the jury, can apply this law to the facts that you have heard, and reach a verdict."

The courtroom became quite still.

"Well, the law is clear. Chapter 279 of the General Laws of Vermont are here before me, and I shall read you Section 6558 of our laws." He made a point to repeat the phrase. "The General Laws of *Vermont.*"

Judge Gleason hooked on his glasses and read to the jury the same paragraph that I had read to myself while sitting in my father's study . . . ending with the part about a guilty defendant being imprisoned from three to twelve months, and fined from $300 to $1,000.

"Or *both,*" Gleason ended his reading, ignoring a rumble from about half of the gallery.

Everyone seemed to lean forward.

"If you find Mr. Lion innocent, he shall go free, at once. But, if the twelve of you agree on his guilt, the defendant must be sentenced by the court. By me."

The jurors looked at each other, as if each one expected some other man to stand up and say something. Yet nobody spoke.

"This," said Gleason, "has not been an easy trial. But I guess I can be allowed to say, based on my years and decades in this building, that *no trial* is easy. Not a solitary one. Most trials have a plethora of hot air, with hardly ever a shortage of hot temper. Nonetheless, we did our jobs, didn't we? We had at it. And, by jingo, now that our job is near finished, I think we can all say that we did our best. We let every citizen speak in turn. Ha! Some even spoke out of turn."

We all reacted. The gallery seeming to be amused as Judge Gleason studied his audience.

"You all out there, the citizens of this town and this county, suffered through breaking in an able young lawyer, a new D.A. and a new judge. The three of us, all being fresh in our positions, stumbled around some. But we somehow, perhaps by Divine guidance, reached the end of the road."

Henry Gleason once again removed his glasses.

"Now, the twelve of you, dear jury, must decide if the defendant is innocent or guilty. I charge you not to be influenced by feelings, one way or another, but only by the *facts* of the case. And it may be painful to you as you decide. Pain is no laughing matter. We are born with it, live with too much of it, and often die in its arms."

With his hands, the judge wiped his face.

"There are *no* easy verdicts. For you, there is not an escape hatch and no simple way out. So many times, in our own personal lives, we find ourselves moving along by making one decision upon another. Day by day. Year in, year out, we grow up and we grow older, having to face an army of matters that beg our deciding, and then having to abide by our own judgments.

"Easy? Heck no. The decision that now confronts each man in this jury is a serious one. Jesse Bolt and I have served as opponents, and nervously waited countless times in this room while Horace Rudder charged the jury. I can't speak personally for Jess, but I sure can own up to all those butterflies that fluttered in *my* stomach. And still do."

My father said, "Indeed."

"None of it's easy, gentlemen. Life is hard. Like cider, perhaps living is harder and sweeter in Vermont than any other place on Earth. Well, life is supposed to be hard, so the weak ones die off. To reach the age of seventy, like me, you got to be damn ornery."

Father nodded.

"Men of the jury, you shall now be excused, and escorted to the jury room, remaining there until you agree on a verdict."

Gleason rapped his gavel.

"This court is now in recess until such time that a foreman is elected by his fellows and a verdict is agreed."

I stood up.

We all did. Watching the twelve jurymen file out the door that was up front, none of them looked happy. Their shirts were sweaty wet, and all their clothes hung upon stooped shoulders that appeared weighted with responsibility.

Two women flanked Petunia Bly. Both were familiar, yet I just couldn't recall their names. Mrs. Bly appeared to be washed out, as if all the starch of Sunday morning had been boiled out of her leaving her limp. Even the flowers on her dress seemed wilted and wan. I wanted to edge my way through the crowd and give her a hug, and I sort of had a hunch that Father wanted to do likewise. I knew how fond he was of Mrs. Bly and that he always wanted to be her friend.

But maybe all that was over.

In pairs, we all filed out of the double doors at the rear of the packed courtroom, outside to the front of our county courthouse. The sun was shining hot, and it made me squint, wondering if there soon would be a break in the weather. The town of Liberty sure could have used a cool breeze.

I spotted Hem. Yet I was sorry to look at him, as his face was now so bitter hard. His arm was half around the shoulder of his mother, Dolly Lion, and next to her he looked to be near twice her size. Walking slowly, the two of them walked to their wagon, surrounded by a pack of Lion men and women who served as a silent escort. Hem saw me, and said nothing but silent hatred.

A voice behind me spoke to someone else. "Well, Charlie, what's going to be the outcome of all this?"

"Blessed if I know."

"Me neither. All I can say is that I don't guess I care for any of it. Not one single bit. Never thought I'd see Jesse Bolt, or anybody else, pound away at that Bly woman."

Listening, I wanted to turn around, as if to tell them . . ., "Hey, I'm his kid. And you're all darn lucky to have a D.A. like my father. Yeah, and a neighbor like Mrs. Bly." But I didn't. Instead, I just moved away, because I didn't want to hear any more chatter on the subject.

Everyone, except for the Lions, seemed to be talking about the trial; some wishing that they were on the jury, while others expressed gratitude that they hadn't been called.

"He's guilty," a person mumbled.

"Pig's eye."

From the corner of my vision, I saw some money changing hands, as three men were nailing down the terms of a wager, arguing about the odds. It made me ill to listen. Yet, I thought, if men would throw dice at the foot of Jesus's cross, over a robe, they'd just about gamble anywhere. About anything.

Father came up to me. He, too, was looking in the direction of the trio of men who were making a bet.

"How could they?" I asked.

"Son, I learned a long time ago that we can't *change* people. The only thing you can do is try to understand them. And by doing so, you'll come to learn a measure or two about yourself."

I nodded. "Are you going to win?"

"That's up to the jury."

"Of course. But what I want to know is, do *you* think you're going to win the case?"

Father shook his head. "No."

"How come?"

"Well, as I look at the situation, it all adds up into one little old word. Fear."

"Fear?"

"People are afraid of what's going to happen to big old Justice. The jury's so nervous that their trousers are wetter than their shirts. Henry's on edge. But then he always is. Mostly, however, it's the jury."

"What are they scared of?"

"It's the Lions."

Rake Tatum limped toward us, cane in hand, taking his own sweet time as he nodded to a few folks.

"Jesse," he said, more like a greeting than the start of a lengthy conversation.

"I suppose," my father said, "you tucked Justice away, Rake."

Sheriff Tatum nodded. "He's back in his cell. This'll give me a breather to stroll home and look in on Miss Penny."

"How's your sister taking all this sticky weather?"

"Better'n most. I know she'd give a day's canning just to be able to come down to the courthouse, and view the trial."

"Reckon so."

"Still and all," Rake said, "I'm just as content she stays put. Especially today. Mind if I walk along with you two gents?"

Father said, "More than welcome."

The three of us were standing just outside the courthouse, near the top step of the five stairs. People were all around us, and I didn't exactly see it happen, but I heard it. Mr. Tatum had sort of turned away to answer somebody's question, while I was looking at Blessing; wanting to say hello to her. I never dreamed that anybody would ever come up to my father and spit in his face. Yet somebody did. Not that I saw it happen. But when my eyes left Blessing and turned back to Father, there it was, a gob of brownish-yellow tobacco spit on his cheek, and smearing his glasses. I never saw who did it. However, I was cocksure that my father had. Father's mouth was open and his body shook.

My fingers tightened into fists as I read the hurt on his soiled face.

I wanted to chase after him, whoever it was, and turn him sorry for what he'd done. My body clenched up tight.

"Easy," said Father.

"But," I said, "some guy just . . ."

"If that's all he did, son, then maybe I got off easy." His voice was quivering as he spoke.

"You don't have to take that."

Rake Tatum turned around. I saw his eyes widen as he got himself a good glance at my father who was wiping off his glasses with a clean white handkerchief. Rake's entire face was a question.

"Who done it, Jess?"

"Forget it."

Right then, I'd have bet a million dollars that my father knew who had spat in his face. Yet he said nothing more. Twisting his head from side to side, Sheriff Tatum looked over the milling crowd. All told, about a quarter of the population of Liberty stood in less than an acre of our village.

"That's a battery," Rake said. "Ain't nobody got a right to spit on a man. Not in my county. Say his name, Jess. I'll nab the lout and jail him."

"Let it lie, Rake. Even though I appreciate your concern, I deem it best that neither you nor I heat up our collars. If this business of Justice Lion's trial ends with no more injury than a stray gob of brown spittle, then let's both count our blessings and kiss it off."

Rake said, "You can press charges for an act such as that, Jess, and you darn well know it."

Father nodded. "I think I can reason *why* I got spat on, and maybe that's enough to generate a bit of forgiveness on *my* part."

"What was the reason, Jesse?"

The three of us started up the street toward home. I walked at Father's right hip while Mr. Tatum flanked the left, and it made me glad that my father was in the middle.

Father said, "The reason was Petunia Bly."

"Figured as much." Rake snorted.

My father smiled. "It's a pleasant thought in a way, Rake, to know that someone else in Liberty loves her more than I do."

Rake Tatum was silent. All I could hear was the slide of his bad foot on the roadway gravel, plus the easy tap of his cane.

"Boy," I said, just to make a noise for myself, "I sure will be thankful when this trial is over. All I do is sit in the gallery and yet I'm plumb worn out."

Rake said, "You, me, and the whole town."

"Henry Gleason was certainly correct about that," my father said, "when he told us that no trial is easy. I pity the jury. Indeed, I truly do."

"How'll it turn out, Jess?"

"Badly."

Sheriff Tatum nodded. "I'd buy that. It's plenty hot back in that jury room right now. They'll all have a lot to spout."

"They'll do it, Rake."

"Always do."

"We've seen plenty, haven't we? All these years and all those trials. You, me, and old Henry Gleason."

Rake Tatum sighed. "It sure did pepper up a quiet summer. And it all got begat when our friend Elmer Sternlock arrived on the scene. Him, and his band of merry men."

I said, "That's from *Robin Hood.*"

"Soldiers of the King," said Father. "The legions of government rarely arrive with glad tidings of joy."

Rake spat. "Jesse, you and I sound like an old pair of fools. Two old bullfrogs croaking in a dark pond, warning the world that things today aren't as sweet as they used to be."

"They never are," said Father. "Our town is destined to change, Rake. You and I and Henry are just relics of yesteryear. Tomorrow belongs to the swift and dapper, like Miles Harvey. And perhaps like Muncie here."

"S'pose so. New faces, new ideas, and a flock of new laws."

Father shook his head. "Prohibition. Next it'll be poker, or music, or a Saturday night barn dance. Guess I wouldn't be surprised if our government levied a tax on spooning in the moonlight with a pretty gal."

I heard Mr. Tatum grunt. "Huh. They probable will, soon as they find out that somebody *enjoys* it. I swallow myself a belt or two, once in a while, and not just to ward off a chill. What's more, badge or no badge, I don't give a rat's rump who knows it."

We stopped just outside our front gate.

"Regards to Miss Penny."

"Thanks. I'll tell her you were asking."

I said, "See ya later, Mr. Tatum."

"Yup. Soon as the jury decides, I'll crank up the contraption and squawk us all back to the courthouse."

He limped away up the street.

We didn't go inside the house right away. I watched my father slump into one of the two rocking chairs on our front porch, his face looking as if he'd crawled through a grinder.

"Tired?"

"Muncie, I'm wrung out. The way I feel now, I couldn't even argue with Henry Gleason. And I'd bet he's not much fresher."

"I'd like to know who was so rotten as to spit in your face. Will you tell me?"

"Yes, providing I have your promise to forgive the gentleman."

"You have it."

"All right, I'll tell you. Because when you hear his name, you'll understand. You will know in your heart why I also forgive him."

"Who was it?"

"Harry Bly."

Chapter 24 ⟨◡⟩

We waited.

Both my father and I had tried to eat a noonday meal, but without much appetite. It was just too hot for fuel.

Father said, "Think I'll stretch out on the couch for a few minutes. Can't seem to keep my eyes open."

"Go ahead. I'll read or something."

"Stay out of mischief."

I promised to.

Up in my room, there was a nifty book that I was almost halfway into, about whales. And on the men and ships that sailed the seas harpooning them, for oil. I was always rooting for the whale. When reading about the bullfights, in Spain, I pulled for the bull. The part I liked most was when the matador got gored. But I didn't feel like reading.

Looking at Father, I saw that he was knocked out, and gently snoring. So I went on tiptoe through the kitchen and out the back door. Gee, I was thinking, what I wouldn't give to spend some time up on Kipp's Mountain, with Hem. And with Blessing.

I headed toward the center of town.

Stores were open. Shoppers were busy, churning the economy of Liberty, stocking up on groceries. As usual, a few wagons waited in front of the feed store, being loaded with dusty bags. Dixon Miller, a kid I was in school with, waved to me and I waved back.

"Hot enough for ya, Muncie?"

"Plenty."

"I s'pose you bottled yourself up in the courthouse all week to watch your pa."

"Yep. Sure did."

"Who's going to win?"

"Beats me," I told him.

"The whole town's talking about Justice Lion. Like nothing else ever happened here. It sure did stir up a ruckus. But I reckon it'll all die down."

"Hope so."

Dix hefted up two blocks of lick-salt for his dairy cows. One was white, the other a light brown, like the color of malt powder that I enjoyed the taste of whenever I spooned some into a glass of milk.

I said, "I just got a nifty idea."

"About what?"

"Well, it's sort of an invention. We ought to invent a block of chocolate malt, so that when your herd of Holsteins lick it, out in the pasture, they all give chocolate malted milk."

"Hey! We'd make a fortune."

"That'd be keen," I said. "Maybe we'd become millionaires. You know, I wouldn't mind keeping a block of malt in the kitchen, or up in my bedroom, so whenever I got nagged by the notion for chocolate, I'd go over and lick it."

Dix made a face. "Trouble is, I don't guess that cows would lick it a whole lot."

"How do *you* know?"

"Well, because we got a cow named Patchwork."

"That's the one you raised up from a calf."

"Yeah, she's my babe. One day I was eating a Hershey bar and broke off a bite to share with her."

"Did she like it?"

"All she did was smell it. And walk off."

I sighed. "There goes our million dollars."

"Maybe," said Dix, "we'll come up with something else. And I hope it's sudden soon, on account I sure get body-sore with farm work. Wish my pa was a lawyer, like yours."

"How come?"

"Well, it seems to me," Dixon said, "that toting a stack of wills around must be a mite lighter than hauling hay."

"Got all your hay in yet?"

Dixon Miller stretched a hand around himself to scratch his back. "Mostly. Sure is blessed hot work. I got enough hayseed inside my shirt to itch me until Christmas."

The way Dix scowled made me smile.

"We're milking sixty head. Plus that, we got a good twenty more, and they eat all winter. Took in our first cut of hay in June. Second cut is ready now and into September. Good crop. Our haybarn's packed right up to the rafters. Not even room enough left for the hornets."

"School starts soon."

"Don't remind me. I still can't figure why I need so much schooling just to be a farmer, like Pa. But my mother says I best go. Ma and Sis are into canning right now, and I'd wager Hell itself is cooler than our kitchen. And whenever my mother is into her cans, I don't guess the Devil himself would dare argue with her."

Dix Miller stopped talking. His face became silent and sober, just before his fist shot up to give my shoulder a friendly farmer's punch.

"I'm sorry, Muncie. I just remembered that you ain't got a ma, and it was dumb stupid of me to howl about mine."

"Forget it."

"Howdy there, Muncie."

"Oh, hi, Mr. Miller. Dixon says you're working him near to skinny. Is that true?"

"Huh. If you ask me," Dixon's father said, "one honest day's work would kill the both of *you* two."

"Pa, I'm next to dead already. Never thought I'd welcome the thought of dragging my bones back to school."

Mr. Miller winked at me. "That's my purpose. And that's why the education folks contrived up a summer vacation . . . to work boys so sweaty that they near to gallop back to their books, come September."

Dix took in a deep breath to sigh out.

"Yessir," his father continued, "I got a son and a daughter to read me the Bible after supper. Even if neither one of 'em listens to what gets spoke of."

They mounted the wagon seat.

"See ya, Muncie."

I watched the team of bays yank the wagon forward, up the road, back home to work a farm. It sort of made me wonder about the Millers. Farmers, I guess, worked harder than most folks. Yet they always seemed to be happier, and healthier. Maybe hard work could both ache a man's body and smile his face.

Things were quiet at the courthouse.

Going around back, I looked into the windows at the jail, until I saw the person I was sort of looking for, and wanted to visit.

"Uncle Justice?"

He looked up. Alone, he sat on his cot, which leaned against the gray wall. Jail didn't appear to be too comfortable a place. Yet it wasn't dirty, or dark. August sunshine drifted in between the bars, making a pattern, strip shadows on the bare concrete floor.

Justice Lion blinked at me. "Who is it?"

"It's me, Muncie."

"Oh. Couldn't see for a spell."

"Are you okay?"

Justice nodded. "I'll abide. Ha! I'd invite you to come in, but right now, there's a legal limit to my hospitality."

I smiled at him. "I sort of wanted to own up to a few things. You know, like explain how everything got . . ."

"Twisted?"

"Yes. By rights, my father would have gladly defended you. If you'd asked."

"I know it."

"He got appointed as the D.A. at a bad time. It couldn't have turned out worse. Even though he's explained it all to me, I don't guess I'll ever understand the machinery of the law."

"Nor I."

"Are you getting fed enough?"

"Too much. Away too generous for a man who don't perform no labor. I leave lots on the plate Rake brings me. Seems like when a man don't work, he don't eat, and there's a Divine righteousness to it."

"You must be really mad inside."

Justice Lion got up from his cot, walking over to the window. "Mad? Well, if'n you mean angry mad, no. As to mad in the head . . ."

"I'd hate to be in a cell." My hand yanked at the iron.

He looked out through the bars, upward, as if searching the trees for a sparrow. "I purchased Dolly a canary one time. At a fair. It lived in a cage. And died there, too. Still it sang."

"That's good."

"When my mind plays with madness, I try to remember our little bird. Her name was Magpie. Pretty and yellow. So I do my level best to sing yellow, and sweet as outdoors."

"Yellow's a happy color."

Justice said, "Aye, it is. When little Magpie died off, we buried her inside a matchbox. Blessing said sweet words over her grave."

"That's real sad."

"Sad, and beautiful. Like life. Right now, boy, me and my family's caught in a storm. A tempest, as some say. Even on a quiet afternoon, like today, I hear the wind up on my mountain, and if I let it happen, that old tempest would tear me to a tatter."

"You and Hem are strong men."

"Ha! Are we? Yester evening, I was in here alone, like usual, looking out and up at the stars, saying words like . . . Lord, you didn't mold me strong enough."

"Well," I said, "if *you're* weak, I sure do pity the rest of us here in Liberty."

"Muncie, they's a passel of people that I pity, in Liberty."

"How come?"

"Because they don't know who they are. Their faces bespeak that their breasts are empty-hearted. Little love in their eyes."

"Your eyes are real blue, like Blessing's."

Justice smiled. "Just now, when you spoke of my daughter, I heard a soft note in your speech. Like your voice could pet her name."

"Reckon you know."

"I do. Me and Dolly both. Some feelings are hard to hide, aren't they?"

"Yes, I guess they are. Whenever you say Dolly, your voice sounds softer than usual."

"I'm proud to admit it."

"I love Blessing."

"Good. She loves you."

"Some ways, it's almost like a hurt. I can't think about anybody, or anything, except Blessing Lion. I say her name over and over."

"A long time back, I did likewise. Only I said Dolly Partridge, Dolly Partridge . . . again and again, and her name would swing to and fro in my bosom, and clang like some golden chime."

"That's almost like poetry. Except it's better because it really is true."

"So be it."

"Darn it, I hate seeing you in a cell!"

"Soft. I won't stay in forever. Besides, I get a herd of visitors. Trouble is, too few of 'em grin. And they all probable wonder why I smile at them. Well, let them think me a fool."

"No one in Liberty or in all of Addison County thinks *you're* a fool. They respect you. Every soul in town."

"Ain't that a caution. Hard for townfolk to admire a man like me who sometimes wears no stockings on his legs. Yet, there's some here I respect, too."

"Like who?"

"Your old pa. I respect Jesse Bolt."

"Thanks. He's home right now."

"To work?"

"No, when I left, he was taking a nap on the davenport."

"Good. Jess wears a washed-out face. I truly believe this trial of mine was hard for him. Perhaps harder than for me."

"Harder than you'll ever know."

"Keep close to him, boy."

"I will."

"Tend his need. Your pa's a lonesome man. Not with an empty heart but with an empty look to his eye. If'n you ask me, he ought to hunt himself up a good-looker of a widow woman, and wed up."

"He won't."

"No, I don't suspect so," he said.

"How come you said that?"

"I knew your mother. Long before she ever knew you. And I can reason why your pa is so alone. Yet he ain't."

"Lots of times he's with her."

Justice nodded his big head. "But you, boy, you're with *him*. The way Hem's with me. My son troubles me some. There's a wild in Hemming. Buck fever."

"I thought buck fever was when a hunter took first sight on a deer and couldn't pull the trigger."

"Hem's trigger will get pulled."

The way Justice said it made me cold. Inside my head, I heard the blast of a shotgun, the same painful noise that rang in my ears on the night I was with Hem, and I was aiming his gun up a tree, to kill a coon.

Justice stared at me. "What ills you?"

"Nothing."

"Don't false me. I can't read a printed word, but a person's face hollers to my ear. So say it out if you're of a mind to. I got time to listen."

"It was about Hem."

"Aye."

"We used to be pals."

"I was grateful to that friendship."

"Makes me wonder if the two of us can ever be friendly again. The way it used to be."

"Boy, nothing is ever the way she used to be. Not in my life, or your pa's. Nary in yours or Hem's."

"I want us to be pals again."

"Moments pass. It'll come in good time, the way a winter melts into spring. We wait it all out, Muncie. You and me. Dolly's waiting, too. Biting her little strong hands. Washing up a cookpot that she already rubbed a rag to."

"I suppose so."

"A sink is a woman's graveside. It's where she stands and spills her grief, so her tears drop to dishwater where they don't telltale a spot."

I was thinking how much I enjoyed listening to Justice Lion talk. His voice was deep, and rich, and yet he could feel so much and for so many. He sure had a temple of a heart.

"You know a lot about people."

"I'm obliged, Muncie. And it's a comfort to my old age to know that at least I could master all that really counts."

"People matter more than law."

"Do you think your pa'd agree to that?"

"Right off," I told him.

"Aye, I'd say he quick would. A pity the two of us, me and your pa, have to tangle this trial on enemy sides."

"That doesn't mean you and Father hate each other."

"Surely don't. Your pa's a stout man, Muncie Bolt, and don't disremember it. He's little and he's lean, but there be a wee fist in him. Not one soul in Liberty doubts that your pa's short on either guts or gizzard."

"Sometimes I wonder what courage is. And if I have any at all."

"Pangs of manhood. So you figure to prove out, and that you best mount up, ride off, and do war with some other young stag. Is that right?"

"Sort of."

"That's my Hem."

"Your son's already grown up."

"Not hardly. Oh, in some ways." Justice Lion dragged a big paw down one of the iron bars of his window. "He tries to be hard, my baby boy. Ofttimes, he's me on the outside, and he's Dolly within."

I nodded.

Justice said, "When nobody's around to take witness, you should see how Hemming cuddles the cat."

"Dearly Beloved."

"Ain't that some handle for a tabby?"

"I bet you miss her."

"Aye. Yet that's not all I miss. A man off a mountain ain't bred to beat his fists on the inside of a jailhouse wall. That's the madness, Muncie. I can weather the morning and the daylight."

"At night what do you do?"

"Everything but sleep."

"Do you pace up and down in there? I would."

"So would any man. Sometimes I ask myself if cooking up a batch of moon was worth all this finery that now encloses me."

"Maybe you'll win."

Justice grunted. "And maybe nay."

I could tell by his face that he was no longer thinking about the trial, but of prison. Being locked up for a long time. Day and night. Busting the walls with his big hands. Feeling his reason shatter, because steel and cement come a lot stiffer than a man's longing to be free.

"Is it hot in there?"

Poking a thick finger at his own chest, he said, "Aye, in *here* it is. Hotter than the cinders of Satan. My whole body's a furnace. Boiling, like the sour-mash corn in the cooker of my whiskey still. The fever's all inside me, boy."

"Are you thinking about prison?"

"Aye, I am. And the thought does me no favor. But if they decide I'm to serve the time, I can hold in my breath for it. I'll have to."

His hand reached through the bars and lightly touched my cheek.

"Muncie, will you do something for me?"

"Of course."

"Stay by Hem. He's my son, with more than a plenty of pride in him. Lion heat and Lion temper. Dolly and Blessing are two I don't fret about. They got sense to be tame."

"But you're worried, aren't you?"

"Only for Hem."

Chapter 25 &

Father sat up.

Looking at me and rubbing his eyes, he asked, "What time is it getting to be?"

"Almost four o'clock."

"Goodness me. I've been asleep for over two hours. Can't believe it." Finding his glasses, he hooked them around his ears, flattening down his thin hair with one casual wipe of his hand.

I said, "You must have needed the rest."

"Guess you're right, son. Did you read?"

"No. I just sort of took a stroll down the street, to see if anything at all was happening."

"Is that all?"

"Well, maybe I went where I had no business going. To tell you the truth, I just had to look in at the jailhouse and to make talk with Uncle Justice."

Father looked squarely at me. "I'm pleased you did, Muncie. However . . ."

"Here it comes, the old red flag."

"Easy now. I don't plan to constantly warn or admonish you. Yet I'd be a rather shabby parent if I didn't harbor *some* concern for your safety and well-being. Agree?"

"S'pose so."

"There are people aplenty in town today. We've hosted strangers all week long. Some that I've never seen before. Others I hardly recognize."

"I guess you're warning me to be careful."

"Quite so. Something's brewing in our atmosphere. I smell it."

"This is a dumb question, but does it have to do with the outcome of the trial? Reckon it does."

Firming his lips, Father nodded. "Yes, and no. Oddly enough, regardless of the verdict on Justice Lion, the nerves of Liberty and Kipp's Mountain are rubbed raw. Twisted. Tighter than a taut rope. It would take very little, son, to touch it off and make it burn."

"I wouldn't do that."

"No, of course you wouldn't. Nor would any other sane citizen ignite such situation . . . intentionally. But best you remember that *you* are my son, and right now, the local D.A. is hardly the shoo-in winner of a popularity contest."

"What are you saying?"

"Not all the Lions are like Justice. Every family spawns its sweet and sour. Good people can, upon provocation, commit an act in haste."

"I have a hunch you saw the shotguns in the wagons outside the courthouse."

"So I did. And I say it's a passel of foolishness. Make no mistake, Muncie. The men who brought those guns *allowed* their weapons to be seen. Flexing their muscles, perhaps."

"Sternlock's men carry guns."

Father nodded. Standing up from the couch, he stretched. And yawned. "Yes, they carry guns. Smith and Wessons. I assume they also enjoy the whispers concerning the obvious bulges beneath their armpits."

"Did you spot a pistol on Elmer Sternlock on the night he came here to talk to you?"

"Of course. Sternlock means business. He's one tough article. The type of man who'd stand up to mobsters in Chicago and use all the federal power available. Lead as well as law."

"There aren't too many people you dislike," I said.

"Why do you presume I dislike Mr. Sternlock?"

"You just do. There's an edge in your voice that you seem to fight to control, whenever you talk about him, or his purposes."

"Quite so. I guess it was his superior attitude toward Rake Tatum that tumbled me over to the opposite side of the fence. And I'd gladly trade *ten* of Elmer Sternlock for just one of old Rake."

"Mr. Tatum's not worried."

"No. Certainly not about anything that Mr. Sternlock says about him. Nor does Elmer scare Henry. Our new judge is a horny old warrior when it comes to combat. It would take more than idle threats to spook Henry Gleason."

"Or to spook you."

"I doubt if I'm that courageous."

"Uncle Justice claims you are."

Father smiled. "Does he now?"

Moving out of our front door, Father and I each took a rocking chair, and sat. It was a muggy afternoon; no wind, and the maple leaves hung in limp fatigue.

"How I wish it would rain," Father said. "Just enough of a downpour to cool things off. And put a damper on dispositions."

"Our lawn looks kind of brown."

Father chuckled. "So do I. And so do we all. Can't remember ever napping for two solid hours in the middle of an afternoon. Had I known, however, that my son was loitering downtown, at the jail, I doubt that I'd have even closed my eyes for a wink."

"Nobody saw me."

"Prut! Somebody saw you for sure. The eyes and ears of a Vermont village seldom relax. Same goes for the tongues. By now, it's all over town that you took yourself to visit Justice Lion."

"So what?"

"Well, as I said before, I'm thankful you did. Loyalty is an admirable quality. But allow me to again remind you, Muncie, that you are also the son of the local D.A. who happens to be prosecuting that particular prisoner."

"I hate to hear Justice called that."

"As do I. Yet you dodge my point. There is, in the law, a term called conflict of interest. Even though you are a schoolboy, there are those in Liberty who might want to draw an improper conclusion as to your visit with Mr. Lion, noble and guileless as it may have been."

"Public opinion never used to pester you."

"Agreed. You're right, son. We can't attempt to steer-wheel our lives through the icebergs of gossip."

I smiled at him. "However . . ."

Father smiled back. "You know me, don't you? However, you and I may both unite on not wanting *anything,* no matter how innocent, to jeopardize or influence this trial. Do you go along with that?"

"You got me."

"Ha! And I am so grateful that I *do* have you. You're my *life* now, son. You and a puny practice of the law. Mostly, it is you, the future Reverend Muncie Bolt."

"I'm sure glad you're not sore about *that.*"

"Not a bit. You can't force a young foot into the wrong boot. You'd feel the pinch and so would I. Upshot, we'd both be limping."

"Good enough."

"Your bugles and banners are yours to pursue, my lad. I vow to you how impossible a task it would be for you to make *me* into a minister. Ha! The hallowed halls would surely come tumbling down. Oh, how I'd savor going to Heaven."

"Why?"

"Think of the living I could earn up where there's bound to be a shortage of lawyers." Father rocked his chair back to laugh at our porch ceiling.

I said, "Lawyers are just as good as anyone else."

"Indeed they be. Just as bittersweet as the rest of the populace. And I imagine we might even dare to place *preachers* on both sides of the line."

"Okay with me." I sighed. "Right now, I'm already on both sides of a trial. Cheering for you and cheering for Uncle Justice. Days like this sure can mix a body up."

"I agree. It was one muddle of a mess. And all over a batch of corn whiskey. But, as our learned county judge so sagely remarked, it was *our* mess. Not that I'm glad I was chosen to slide into all the muck. Yet, in a way . . ."

"You'd hated to be left out."

"I confess. I truly admit I'm rather proud to be a new D.A. and to play a part. Proud of Henry Gleason, proud of young Miles, of Rake . . . and of Justice Lion."

"And I'm proud of you."

Father stopped rocking to look at me. As though he wanted to say words that he couldn't say. So I thought I'd just jump in and bail him out. "I'm proud that you raised such a fine son."

His face brightened. "So am I. Ha! Oh, it's good to laugh. Better yet to start liking myself once again. Lately, I have honestly been hating my own bowels. Even, so help me Hannah, loathing the law. At last I can hold up my head again and go back to hating dear old Henry."

"Pig's ear. You don't hate Mr. Gleason and he doesn't hate you. It's a small town, and all these years you and he were opposing lawyers. That's all."

"Two old bobcats spitting in a closet." Father laughed. "Scrapping over one bone."

"That's the legal profession for you. Now you know why I'm going to be a minister. There won't be any arguments."

"Ho ho! Are *you* in for a picnic. I can hardly wait until the board of deacons and the choir and the ushers and the Sunday school teachers, not to mention every oddball opinion in the entire congregation, digs their claws into *your* Sunday best."

"Really?"

"Really. I'll probably receive a telegram saying that you vaulted out of your pulpit and headed straight for Harvard Law School."

"Not likely," I told him.

We were still laughing when we looked up to see the approach of Sheriff Tatum. He was walking as fast as I had ever seen him travel.

"Any news, Rake?"

"They're all done, Jess."

My behind felt frozen into the chair. I couldn't budge. But my father was already on his feet, inside the front door, fetching his coat and hat and briefcase.

"What's the verdict going to be, Mr. Tatum?"

Rake shook his head. "Hard to say. A jury'll sometimes do strange. I got my own personal hopes, which best I keep quiet about, seeing as I'm a hunk of it all. Sorry business."

The three of us walked down the street, into the village proper, toward the county courthouse. People were quiet. The sun had ducked behind a rather large dark cloud, causing the sky over Liberty, Vermont, to become as somber as most of the faces I saw. In the distance, from beyond Kipp's Mountain, I heard the threat of thunder.

I remembered Blessing and me, in the rain.

As soon as the two big doors were unlocked, we all filed slowly inside, where I noticed how people seemed to sit in exactly their previous seats. Same row and same spot. I took a deep breath. Damn! Now I didn't know which side to choose, whether to sit behind Uncle Justice, or back of Father. So I didn't sit at all. I just stood in the open doors.

"All rise."

Judge Gleason, wearing his black robe, entered the courtroom by his up-front door. For a man his age, he really bustled like a bee, and looked as though he wanted to sting somebody. Or everybody. He rapped his gavel.

"Please be seated."

The twelve men of the jury already sat in the jury box. No one was smiling. All were silent. Fact is, never had the courtroom appeared to be so quiet.

"At this time," said Judge Gleason, "I wish to express my sincere thanks, as well as the gratitude of our community, to the jury. As the twelve of you well represent the diverse sentiments of Addison County, the court implores that we all abide by the decision that you have reached, in good faith."

Quietly we waited.

"Gentlemen of the jury," asked Gleason, "have you all reached a verdict?"

Lyman Rayno, acting as foreman, stood up from his seat in the jury box. "Yes we have, your honor."

Turning toward the table where Justice sat, Judge Gleason asked, "Will the defendant please rise and face the jury?"

Justice Lion stood.

As did everyone else in the room, I then whipped my attention over to where Mr. Lyman Rayno stood, wiping his face with a rumpled bandana. He didn't seem to enjoy being a juror and wouldn't look anywhere except down at his own shoes.

"Well?" snapped Gleason.

Mr. Rayno cleared his throat. "Your honor . . ."

"Yes?"

Pausing a moment, Lyman Rayno fumbled a hand into the pocket of his shirt in order to produce a crumpled piece of white paper, from which he then slowly read to us, in a wavering voice.

"Your honor, if it please the court, we of the jury find Justice Lion, the defendant . . . guilty as charged."

From all over the courtroom, I heard "No" after "No." Heads were shaking as if to erase what Mr. Rayno had said. My father wasn't smiling. Only looking downward at his hands that were finger-locked across his shirt front.

"Thank you, Mr. Rayno," said Gleason. "You may sit."

A "No" or two persisted, until Henry Gleason whacked his gavel to demand our return to order. Justice faced him, waiting.

Gleason sighed. "Very well. Now it is the duty of this court to pass sentence. However, before I do, is there anything that you, Mr. Lion, wish to say?"

Justice shook his big shaggy head.

"Considering our verdict," said Gleason, "and based upon the Laws of Vermont, I will not require that the defendant pay a fine. Times are hard enough. Instead, I sentence him to serve in the state penitentiary for a term of one year."

Gleason banged his gavel as hard as he could hit, as if he hated his big judge's desk. "This case of People versus Lion is hereby closed."

The court nearly burst with noise. I noticed that Elmer Sternlock and his two men stood up quickly as if to insure that Judge Gleason left the courtroom unharmed. One of the men left with him. Sternlock was smiling, offering a congratulatory hand to my father, who hesitated, then took it.

Rake Tatum stood at Justice's side, reaching up a bony hand to pat the bigger man on his shoulder. Justice stood so still that I thought he was stanchioned. Pegged into the floor. I saw Justice's head turn slowly to look at Father; and then he, too, extended his hand. Mr. Tatum was facing me, so that I could see my father on one side and Uncle Justice on the other.

Everyone was talking, or shouting. People were yelling to other people and the men who had bet money on the trial's outcome seemed hungry to collect. Miles Harvey shook hands with my father, too. So did Rake.

It wasn't going to be easy to work my way forward through all the people, because it was sort of like being a small salmon trying to swim up a heavy stream. I was pushing against the crowd. Lots of folks, it seemed, had to get home by chore time, to either start supper or feed the stock. I couldn't see Blessing or Hem.

"Fork over," I heard a man say to some luckless gent who must have put down a wager on the defense. The rumpled cash changed hands almost under my nose and it darn near made me want to throw up. Or punch the guy in the nose. But hurting somebody wouldn't help much or prove anything. Besides, there had already been enough pain, plus maybe more to follow, including prison.

The Lions were not all in a group, but rather dispersed, as everyone in the gallery inched toward the back of the courtroom while I was still trying to get up front.

I heard the word "Later." And then another man said something about waiting until dark.

When I finally wormed my way to the forward floor of the courtroom, there was Father. I shook his hand. "Congratulations," I said. Saying it made me happy for him but I felt rotten about Justice Lion's having to go to jail. Still and all, as my father had told me earlier, there might be an appeal, if Mr. Harvey could convince Justice that there was any possibility of reversing the ruling. From the evidence, I doubted that there was any chance at all.

"I'm sorry," I told Uncle Justice, because I didn't know what else to say. My pity must have sounded lame to a man headed for prison.

"Don't blame your pa, boy," said Justice. "It weren't the hands of Jesse Bolt that built my still and thumped my barrels. It be I. So I'll swallow the medicine. And don't let no man tell you it weren't a fair trial. I figure I got an honest shake."

I also told Mr. Harvey that I was sorry about the outcome. To my surprise, his eyes were really red. Up close, he didn't look a whole lot older than I was. Maybe not even twenty-five. He easily could have passed for Henry Gleason's grandson.

"Who are you?" he asked, smiling. "Say, aren't you . . ."

"I'm Muncie Bolt. And if it's okay with you, sir, I feel like crying about as much as you do."

Miles Harvey sighed. "Next time," he said, "I'll know better. We didn't have a prayer."

Father said, "Son, let's go home."

Justice and Rake Tatum stood side by side and I heard Uncle Justice say, "Home. Home's a good place to go."

Chapter 26 ❧

I t was getting dark.

Father and I had eaten very little for supper, as neither of us were too hungry. I kept sighing, thankful that it was over, and that the case was decided.

"Let's sit out on the porch, shall we?"

"Okay," I said.

He took one rocker and I slumped myself down in the other. The town was still, except for a choir of crickets, all of whom seemed to keep on debating the points of the trial, arguing in the twilight. Over west, beyond Kipp's Mountain, the pink was fast fading to gray, as though it was burning to ashes. A sorry sky.

Someone was coming.

The man didn't seem to be in too much of a rush, just strolling. Approaching our house, he paused, turning in at the front gate. He waved a hand to us.

"Anybody to home?"

It was Judge Gleason.

Father said, "Henry, what a surprise. I figured you'd be tucked away in bed by now, where all decent folks ought to be."

As our smiling visitor mounted our front steps, I vacated my chair. Father stood up, too. Henry Gleason looked worn out. "Thank you, Muncie. Don't mind if I do seat myself. These bandy old legs aren't made for standing up too much. Not anymore."

He and Father occupied the twin rocking chairs, while I sat on the top stair, leaning my back against one of our white porch posts.

My father groaned. "It's over."

"Hah!" Gleason snorted. "Funny, but those are the very words you just took out of *my* mouth. Yessiree, she's ended, Jess. And I hope we did her up brown."

"So we did, Henry."

I kept quiet; not caring to talk, but wanting very much to hear what these two older men were going to say to each other. For some reason, I had started to like Mr. Gleason a whole lot. And I felt glad that he'd walked over to our house, this evening, to pay us a social call.

"Any ideas, Jess?"

"On what?"

"You know damn well . . . on what. The trial, the findings of the jury, and my sentence that I slapped on Justice."

Father said, "A tall order."

"'T' is."

"So, Henry, do you want to discuss your three questions in order? If so, I guess we start on the trial."

"Dang it. You're no doubt as sick of it all as I am. But I've *got* to review it, Jess, while it's all still fresh in my mind. And yours."

"I understand."

"Good."

"The fact is, your honor, I can't imagine my thinking or talking about anything else. Leastwise, not tonight. And I'm glad you dropped over."

"Can that *your honor* crap. Especially in the light of how you and I have more colorfully tagged one another over the years."

Father laughed. "Done. Hank, you ran a tolerable good trial."

"You know, it's been awhile since you've called me Hank. Not since you dropped out of our poker game."

"Guess I started calling you other names."

Henry Gleason's old voice cackled out a laugh, seeming to enjoy the combat. "Some of those handles I well deserved."

225 ❧

"As to the trial," said Father, "it moved right along, thanks to your personal aversion for hot weather and long winds . . . except for your own."

"I'll ignore the dig. What else?"

"The admission of evidence, as you know, is always a sticky business. And both Mr. Harvey and I submitted our full measure. Including, of course, my hunks of copper from Justice Lion's still."

"That," grunted Gleason, "I could take. But, good grief, when you hauled in those bags of sugar, Jess . . ."

"Don't complain. Remember, I've worked plenty in that courtroom and have seen you do worse."

"Worse than *sugar* sacks? Come now."

"You must be slipping, Henry. Don't tell me you've forgotten the Amaden case, the time you led in Folger Amaden's jackass."

Gleason slapped his own knee. "Oh, that one. Slipped my mind, as I've been hoping the town *and* the county would forget that."

"No, no. We well recall. That was the day I thought old Horace Rudder was going to make you eat that jackass, hoof and all."

"He darn near did. Boy, old Horace was a corker, wasn't he? You and I never got away with too many of our tricks."

My father smiled. "We tried."

"You know," said Gleason, "when Folger's jackass disgraced himself, dumping his stinking droppings on the courtroom floor, Horace fined me for contempt. That old cactus."

"Easy now. There's a young attorney in the county by the name of Miles Harvey, plus one or two more coming along, that'll refer to you this evening as that old cactus called Henry Gleason."

The judge snorted. "Is that what I've become?"

"Nay." Father held up his hand to protest the other man's words. "You've *always* been a cactus. Now that you have a robe and gavel, you'll be the prickly pear we all expect."

The two lawyers were quiet for a moment, the two chairs rocking in unison. It was a harmonizing movement.

"We're astray from our subject, the trial."

"So we are. I'm grateful for more than one moment."

"Such as?"

I saw Father reach over and and gently touch the old judge's hand. He patted it, just once.

"Henry, I'm glad you stood up to Elmer Sternlock, and equally content with how you didn't shove Rake into a corner, about his geographical testimony."

"He had me, on Constitution."

"Yes, he did. Furthermore, we all appreciated your allowing young Hemming Lion to read his father's landgrant."

Gleason sighed. "That was impressive."

"Quite."

"Jess, of all the documents we oft listen to in a courtroom, there are doggone few that conclude with the seal and signature of a British king."

"George Rex."

Henry Gleason stamped his heel on our porch floor. "Damn it. I didn't want or covet any of this trial. If it hadn't been for Elmer Sternlock's breathing his federal wind down my collar, and muscle from Montpelier, I might well have dismissed the charges, slapped Lion with a puny little fine, and told Rake Tatum . . . off the cuff, of course . . . that he and I would run Addison County as we dang well please."

"Volstead won't let you do that, Judge."

"I know that. The good old days are over. At least for a while and maybe even for good. Or for evil."

My father said, "Times change."

"The Hell they do, Jesse. Times don't change at all. Somehow, they only up and quit."

"You sound like you're feeling elderly." As my father spoke, he twisted his head to look at Mr. Gleason. The judge shook his head, and grunted. "Elderly? Compared to you, I'm close to twenty years senior. And next to our young Mr. Harvey, I'm not elderly at all. I'm a geedee *fossil*."

Father hacked out a laugh. "Well, dear old fossil, did the verdict surprise you?"

"All verdicts surprise me. And every time I'm positive of one, sure as shooting, they parade in with just the opposite."

"Tell me, Henry, how would you like to have prosecuted that case?"

"Hmm. If a defendant's a rotten apple, I don't lose any sleep after I help freight the rascal off to prison. Nary a wink. But this case haunts the hell out of me."

"How so?" asked Father.

"Well, it isn't just because Justice Lion is basically a good man. Trouble is, we now are playing host to the Washington boys, not to mention a few in the state house. We don't need so much intervention in Liberty, or in Addison County, or in all of Vermont. I wish they'd all mind their own sweet business and let us mind ours." Gleason's little fist pounded the arm of the rocker.

"I well imagine the Lions feel likewise."

"Right you are. But I'll be busted if every Lion ever born is going to stampede me or my court. To tell you the truth, Jess, as soon as I saw all the shotguns and their show of strength, it girdled my guts."

"So that explains why you threw a year at Justice."

"Possibly so. He was guilty as sin. Even said as much. But if I'm going to fill Horace Rudder's boots, I can't sing scared, Jess. If the Lions thought they could lean on my court, my jury, or on any witness, they now have themselves and their scatterguns another blessed think."

Father lightly punched Mr. Gleason's shoulder. "Bully for you."

"I hate myself for that sentence. Even though the old gent may get his term reduced for good behavior, it's still a long time to serve, in the light of such a minor infraction. Justice Lion didn't draw off the first run of whiskey in those hills and I surely hope it won't be the last. Maybe, if the Lion clan had boycotted the trial and stayed away from the courthouse, I would have backed off. Three months. Or even fined the old buzzard a hundred bucks and told him to scat home and keep his nose clean. And hide his next still in a more secluded cranny."

"Perhaps you should have," said Father.

"Then, if I can take into account your tone, you thought the sentence was a mite excessive. Too heavy?"

"I'm not the county judge. You are."

"Bosh. During all those years that I was prosecuting, you were judging my efficiency as the D.A. in this county. Don't tell me that *you,* of all people, plan to quit being *my* judge."

"I'm biased, Henry. Oh, I wanted to win this one. Yet I was hoping that if I was lucky enough to get a verdict, *you* might suspend."

"Suspend?" snapped Gleason.

"You could have, you know."

"Of course I *could* have. And soon as I did, the upstate gents would whip their knives out, maybe for both of us. Want a confession, Jess? I *want* this judgeship. Boy, I've wanted it for twenty years, and it started back before old Horace Rudder began to cough."

"You're honest to say so. So I'll be just as bare-faced, if the court will allow, and tell you how much being D.A. means to me."

Both of the men looked my way, for some reason; perhaps because I was smiling at both of them. I sure enjoyed their talking.

"Muncie," said Judge Gleason, "ignore whatever your father tells you and *never* read for the law."

"I won't, sir," I said, hoping that Father wouldn't blurt out that I was planning to become a preacher.

"Good," said Gleason.

Looking at Father, I shook my head, so that he'd know I wanted my future plans to be secret for awhile, and not jabbered all over town. He understood. My old man was a sharp article when it came to looking inside Muncie Bolt.

"Say," said Father, "would you care for something to wet your whistle? I still have a half a jug of spirits inside, and I reckon we deserve a swig."

Henry Gleason patted his stomach. "We sure do. Trouble is, my insides can't take booze anymore. Not like the old poker days. What I'd really enjoy is a good cup of tea."

"Fine," said Father.

Jumping up, I said, "I'll get it. The kettle's probably still pretty hot from heating the dishwater, after supper. Won't take me a jiffy."

Father asked Judge Gleason what he usually took in his tea.

"Oh, about half a teaspoon of sugar. Maybe a drop or two of lemon, if it's handy. Or vinegar."

I said, "Coming right up."

Poking up the kitchen stove, I nudged the teakettle over the hottest griddle, then removed two of our best china cups and saucers from the cupboard. I figured that a level spoon of tealeaves in each cup was about right, as usual. Then I added sugar. We didn't have any lemon.

I thought I'd heard thunder.

Looking out through the curtains over the sink, I couldn't see any lightning, even though the stars weren't yet visible. No moon. Well, if a storm was coming, we sure would be blessed by a good hard rain. The noise came again, louder, a roll of sound that grew and grew; yet it didn't seem to come from our back yard.

Something sure was strange.

Not bothering to stand around our kitchen to wait for the water to boil, I went outside on the front porch to where Father and Judge Gleason were leaning forward in their rockers. Whatever the sound was, it sure wasn't on our street. Yet nearby.

"Sounds like an anxious wagon," Judge Gleason said.

"Over on Summer Street," I said, pointing over the roof of the Larkins' house across the way.

"Whoever they be," said Gleason, "I got a hunch they're in some kind of a hurry."

As he spoke, I heard the teakettle start to hiss, the way it always did prior to its water boiling. But instead, I listened for the wagon, hearing it turn a corner in town and then head up our street, coming our way. Squinting, I saw two mules yanking a buckboard wagon, pounding the dust in the road to a full let-out gallop. I felt my father's hand on my shoulder.

"Go inside, Muncie."

As he quickly pushed me back toward our front door, the buckboard rattled by our house. I saw the two mules being whipped by the man who was holding the reins in one hand. And a sudden orange puff.

Then I heard the shotgun.

I heard it roar, just after my leg felt as if I'd been stung by the world's biggest and meanest hornets. Judge Gleason's body spun around, twisting, as if he was dancing some crazy dance. And my father pitched forward, down our porch stairs, and onto the front walk.

A man's voice yelled something. Ears back, the mules hurried the wagon uproad, out of sight, and headed out of town.

"Jesse!"

It was Henry Gleason who hollered. As he bumped against me, the two of us half stumbled and half fell down our porch stairway. Father lay on his back. His shirtfront wasn't white anymore. As I touched the cotton, my hand felt hot and sticky. There was blood all over my fingers.

"Father?"

Judge Gleason was down on his knees, lifting up my father's head. My legs were really hot, as if I was standing in some kind of fire, and it was burning me up from inside. Yet I knew I was near to all right. Mr. Gleason's breathing was heavy and husky. And my father wasn't moving. His eyes were wide open, looking up at a dark sky.

"Jesse? Oh, for God's sake."

"Is he . . ."

Bending low, Henry Gleason rested his ear close to my father's chest, listening. I could hear nothing except for the whistle of the teakettle coming from our kitchen stove. As if it was screaming.

"Jess. Jess!"

My father opened his lips, saying no words.

"It was the Lions," said Henry Gleason to my father's almost-motionless face. "I know that brace of mules. One's got a white stocking. Lion mules."

"My . . . chest . . ."

"Lie still, Jesse. Don't try to move. Muncie, get some rags. No, wait. Hurry down the road and fetch Mrs. Bly."

I ran. My legs didn't run too well, and everything I looked at seemed to exist in twos and threes. All a blur. Even before I got to her house, only a few doors away, I was yelling.

"Mrs. Bly! Mrs. Bly!"

She was running toward me, arms out. "My Lord, I heard it. Went right by. What's the trouble? Get back inside, you kids! Do as I say now. Come on, Harry."

"Mrs. Bly, my father's been shot."

She screamed into my face. I stumbled against her big warm body and she held me close to her.

"No," she said. "No, not Jesse Bolt."

"He's . . . all bloody. Can you come?"

We ran. Never before did I imagine that Mrs. Bly could travel that rapidly through the dark. Yet she did. We got back in a matter of a minute. Some of our other neighbors were coming, too.

Judge Gleason looked up. "Petunia, it's Jess."

"I know. . . . I know. The boy said he got gunshot. How bad is it?"

Mrs. Bly knelt down on the grass in our front yard, her fingers searching Father's wrist for a pulse. Other people came and brought a lantern. When I saw all the blood spatter I just about passed out cold. Arms reached out to hold me up and then lay me down on the grass. My ears were ringing which made me wonder if it was the teakettle.

"Jesse?"

I heard Father say her name. "Petunia?"

"Yes, I'm right here. Fetch that lantern in closer. Good. That's it. Lie easy now, Jesse, and let me cut away your shirt. Are you saying something?"

"Petunia . . . I'm sorry."

Chapter 27 ❧

Two of the neighbors carried my father into the house.
There were plenty of people around to help out, but I knew it wouldn't take but one man to carry Father. Lying on our parlor couch, he looked so frail; more like a sick child than a dying man.

"Somebody fetch Doc Rickover."

"Can't. Doc's out of town."

"When'll he be back?"

"Tomorrow."

I heard Judge Gleason say, "Jesse Bolt won't wait for tomorrow. Unless we stop his bleeding, he maybe won't even wait until midnight."

Looking down, it was then that I noticed my own shoes. Both were a deep red. Blood-soaked. Pulling up my torn trousers, I saw that my legs were just as red, and as runny. Burning up hot. Yet I was alive. I couldn't feel my legs. It was as if I wasn't even living from about the knees down. Sort of numb.

Mrs. Bly said, "Somebody boil me some water."

I wanted to throw up. My mouth tasted supper for a second time, bitter and acidy, as if everything inside me was about to bubble up mean. I heard Mrs. Bly comforting Father.

"Blood's a messy business. But lots of times, there's plenty more bleeding than there is hurt. Jesse, you're some speckled up. Had it been a slug, or buckshot, you'd be blasted wide open raw."

"What was it?" somebody asked.

"Scatter." Mrs. Bly washed my father's chest with a red cloth, and I saw all the purple holes. "More than a score. And to make it worse, old Jess here don't carry much meat on his bones, to ward off."

I asked her, "Just how bad is it?"

"Bad enough, boy. But the more holes there be, the better it is for your pa. Oh, he took near a full load of the little devils. He's wearing lots of lead."

"Deep?"

"Well, deeper than chigger bites."

Mrs. Larkin, our neighbor from across the road, was tending Judge Gleason, and trying to gently peel off his shirt. I heard her voice.

"Settle still, Henry."

"Damn it, don't order me about. I won't sit still and you can't . . ."

"Hold him, Herman, and calm him down."

I couldn't stand up. For some reason, my lower leg muscles weren't working. Either that, or they just up and quit, and I sort of crumbled down to the parlor floor. I heard Father trying to say something.

"Petunia . . . I . . ."

"Hush up, Jess. Now then, fetch me a pair of them needle-nose pliers, from the drawer this side of the sink. In with the cook spoons. Jesse, you got yourself punctured up worse than proper."

"Here."

Mrs. Bly's hand grabbed the pliers, squinted at them, and made a face. "They're dirty. Go dunk 'em in boiling water and don't dry off the jaws on the seat of your pants, Harry. Wave 'em dry in the weather, hear?"

"Do . . . my son . . ."

"Lie still, Jesse. The boy's all right."

I didn't tell anybody about how much my lower legs were hurting, because I wanted Father tended to first, along with Mr. Gleason. But my shins were burning.

My father's trying to talk was a good sign.

"Get some whiskey."

Lifting up my father's head, they poured a jug drink, and then two more of the same, into my father's throat. He coughed.

"Enough."

Piercing into his chest, the twin legs of our pliers were silvery, but coming out, both were a shiny red, and holding a tiny ball of lead between the lips. My father groaned.

"I . . . guess I'm a coward . . ."

"No," said Mrs. Bly, "you ain't. Agony of the flesh is hardly a picnic, so don't expect much jolly in it. Lie easy. This one's bedded."

"Jesus."

"Go ahead. Pray all you need to, Jess. And I say," Mrs. Bly grunted as she worked, "it's high time you took up with the Almighty, as He's good company."

"Amen." I heard Mrs. Larkin add, "You're next" to Judge Gleason.

Ball by ball, out of my father's chest they came; Mrs. Bly never stopping until she'd probed and picked at every purple hole. As she worked, I held Father's hand, feeling his pain each time his thin fingers sprang at my own. It made me close my eyes, and whisper to Heaven that he'd pull through. Looking up, I saw Father force a grin at Mrs. Bly, and then ask her a question. "Good grief, Petunia, what in merry Hell are you using? A spade?"

"Damn you, Jess."

Father groaned. "I knew you'd find a way to get even with me. So enjoy your nurse-maiding."

"Jesse Bolt, if you think for one blessed second that a shotgun is my kind of revenge . . ."

I saw her nip at his belly with an unnecessary bite of the pliers. It made me half smile and half cry. Because it felt so good to know that the Blys and the Bolts were still friends, and always would be, forever.

"I'll fix *you*," Mrs. Bly warned my father. Reaching for a bottle of alcohol, she splashed it down on his chest, making him scream.

"That's it. Holler out the poison. You don't fix to fester up, do you?"

Father moaned. "Thank you, Petunia."

"For what? Just for saving your worthless hide so's you can cut mean again, at good folks in a courtroom. Some district attorney *you'll* be. Worse'n old Henry."

Father squeezed my hand. "Muncie?"

"I'm right here."

"He's right fine, Jess, so don't you . . . Mary and Joseph, look at that boy's legs!"

"I'm okay," I tried to tell her.

"No, you're not."

Pushing me down on the floor, Mrs. Bly yanked off my shoes, socks; and, before I could stop her, she tore up both cuffs of my trousers. Then it became *my* chance to holler at the hands that were holding me, feeling the gnaw of the pliers as they bit into my flesh. I kicked.

"Don't you *dare* hoof at *me,* you little demon, or I'll roll you over and tan your butt." Mrs. Bly shook a fist at me.

"Stop it. Ow!"

"Hold yourself still. Sit on him, Harry. And if'n he kicks me again, whack him senseless."

Harry Bly's breath was strong. As he wheezed into my face, I tried to turn my head to the side to avoid smelling. My ear felt the roughness of our frayed rug. When the alcohol hit my legs, I yelled out, and called Mrs. Bly the worst name I could think of.

Leaning down, she kissed my sweaty face.

"And I favor you, too, Muncie."

My arms grabbed her around the neck as I tried not to cry. "I'm glad."

She held me.

"So am I, boy. Glad, sorry, dead, and alive. Don't you fret. Your mean-mouth old pa is a tough potato. He's got plenty behind his belly button. Even if he oughta take his briefcase and stick it up where the moon don't shine."

I saw her scowl at her husband. "Harry, go home and take your-self a bath. You smell worse'n a wet dog."

Mr. Bly smiled back at his wife.

"Now then," said Mrs. Bly, "it gives me great pleasure to an-nounce to you, Judge Gleason, it's *your* honorable turn."

"No."

"What do you mean, *no?*"

"I'm only stung. Besides, they said Doc'll be back tomorrow, so I'm waiting for . . ."

Mrs. Bly told him, "The dickens you are. Hold him down."

"Petunia, don't you *dare.*"

"Ha! I dare more than that, you old goat. Harry, lock our judge down proper, so's I can bathe him, and let out his lead."

Henry Gleason hooted and hollered, using some terms that were unfit for a county judge, or even a sewer rat. He sure could swear. One long string of old favorites followed another, but Mrs. Bly seemed to be deaf to his pithy protests. Her pliers were, too. Out came the lead along with the cussing. I saw Mrs. Larkin raise up her hands to cover her ears. Mr. Gleason mentioned God a few times.

"That's it, Henry," said Mrs. Bly. "About time you returned to expressing your thanks. And it's also high time somebody in this town, mainly *me,* got even with you two old buzzards for trying Justice."

Henry Gleason hollered louder. I reckon the alcohol didn't im-prove his disposition a whole lot.

Father looked pale. I was hoping that he'd try to sit up, but no. He just stared upward at the paint that was curling off our old ceiling.

"Blood," said Mrs. Bly. "I'd rather butcher a pig than work on you three birds. That's the trouble with men. Dish'em a lick of pain and they think it's Kingdom Come."

Gleason snorted. "Damn easy for *you* to say."

"Is it now? Well, the bleeding flushes out the wound. Nature's way. Jesse tapped a bucket of blood, but a puddle of bleeding always looks to be worse than it is. Somebody fetch me that jug."

"No!" Henry Gleason yelled. "You're not dumping any of that on *me*."

Mrs. Bly grunted. "Who gives a rat's rump about *you*." Raising the jug to her lips, she helped herself to a healthy series of swallows, wiping her lips on the blood-stained sleeve of her faded dress.

My father's mouth twitched at a grin. But then his face hardened with pain, closing his eyes, tightening his hand into mine. I could almost feel how much his body was smarting.

"I'll get even," I said to him.

Opening his eyes, he slowly rolled his head to look at me. "No . . . you won't. It's over, Muncie, so let it rest."

Gleason muttered. "Over, my foot."

"Yes," Father said in a soft voice. "Please . . . let it all be over and done with. For my sake. And . . . for the peace of the town."

Mrs. Bly nodded. "As I see it, the Lions didn't cotton to take their full vengeance. Bad enough, but it could have been a lot worse than a barrel or two of duckshot. They weren't shooting to kill cold."

"No," said Judge Gleason, "I don't guess they were. All I can say is this. The Lions wanted to hurt us because of what Jesse and I did to their patriarch. We hurt Justice, they figure, so an eye for an eye. Petunia, you're right. Whoever it was, they didn't aim to cut down any one of us."

"Humf!" Mrs. Bly grunted. "If you want *my* opinion about this horror, somebody ought to march right down to the jailhouse, and report the whole business to Justice."

Father shook his head. "Petunia . . . please don't."

"And why not?"

"Because," my father almost whispered, "learning about our getting gunshot would hurt Justice Lion more than it hurt us."

Mrs. Bly nodded. "True. It'd painful him some."

Using clean rags, she bandaged the three of us; Father, me and

Judge Gleason. I felt a prickly feeling returning to my legs; and it made lying still almost impossible; like I wanted to jump around to stomp out a flame.

Somebody took Henry Gleason home.

At the kitchen sink, I drank almost three full dippers of water. The fire was in my throat as well as my legs. Mrs. Bly and Mrs. Larkin started working on our couch and the parlor floor, with pans of soapy water, and scrub brushes. Other people left to go home and to bed. I sure didn't feel very sleepy.

Father lay on the couch in our parlor, eyes closed, breathing gently in and out. Sometimes his face would twitch, which made me realize that he wasn't too comfortable. Yet we were all alive.

Turning, I saw Rake Tatum and his cane come through the front door and enter our parlor. He spoke. "Evening. I just heard what happened down here. We been busy uproad, at the accident. Doc Rickover here?"

"No. He's out of town." Mrs. Bly raised up erect but still on her knees. "What accident?"

"A wagon took a header. The dang fool was whipping his mules through town and cut a corner too sharp. Front wheel busted up against a watering trough and it throwed out the driver."

"Is anybody . . ."

Rake nodded. "Wagon crushed him."

Listening, I edged a step closer to the couch where Father was resting. He looked near to sleeping and didn't even open his eyes. Sheriff Tatum walked to the couch, looked at my father, and then lightly touched his hand.

"Your pa's all right?"

"He's been shot," I said. "Judge Gleason, too."

"I'm sorry, Muncie. When your pa wakes up, tell him I was asking."

I said I would. Mrs. Bly stood up. "What about the accident, Rake?"

"If you're through here, Petunia, best you come. And quick."

"Go along," said Mrs. Larkin. "I'll keep here with Jesse and the boy. And finish up."

"I'm coming too," I said.

Outside it was pitch dark. Yet up and down the street, lights were burning in several of the homes, and more than one porch held conversation.

"I was abed," said Mr. Tatum. "And then I heard Miss Penny call out and wake me up. Said there was a disturbance. So I got my clothes on, and come."

We walked as quickly as possible. Mrs. Bly was faster than Rake's limp and my wounded legs, but we hurried. Voices waited for us.

"They say," Rake told us, "them two mules run off, heading uproad, and dragging a busted buckwagon clear out of town. T' was better'n full dark when I got there. Couldn't see who the injured party was."

Inside, my mind was yelling at me . . . *no,* I don't want to find out, because I'm afraid I already know.

Three people held lanterns. Below, in the dust of the road, I saw the ruts. Several deep scars in the dirt that were freshly cut by a turned-over buckboard. Wood splinters and a hinge of rusty iron covered the ground. Inside the ring of people lay a fallen man. Even though his clothing was torn into tatters, and bloodsoaked, there was a smell to him that I knew. I could tell right away quick who it was.

Hem Lion.

"Mrs. Bly's here," someone said.

"Let her through, folks."

"Maybe we best cart him inside to a lamp."

"No," said Petunia Bly, "don't budge him. I'll need shears, clean blankets, hot water, a pint of alcohol, and some white rags or old bed sheets that are fresh-out washed. And hasten up."

Hem was motionless. So still that I trembled to look at him.

Beneath his twisted body lay the shiny stock of a shotgun, the same one that I'd used to miss a coon. A hundred years ago, when we were still boys, I thought. Last week. Or was it the week before? I just stood and stared down at Hem. My legs weren't hurting so much now. Maybe because my heart was so cramped. This broken boy wasn't just anyone. He was my best friend.

We washed him. Mrs. Bly did most of it while I helped, handing her things; and using the shears where she ordered me to, cutting away Hem's clothing that was stiff with a mixture of dried blood and road grit. Odd, but I felt Hem's pain. It cut me again and again.

I saw white things, shiny, jutting out from Hem's chest. Broken ribs. Easing off his trousers, my hand touched the wet coils that were steamy and hot, and slippery. I had never touched bowels before.

"He's ruptured," Mrs. Bly said.

The two of us washed Hem and wiped him, but the blood wouldn't stop. The bleeding gushed out of him and soaked into the underneath dirt.

Hem was trying to talk.

"More light," Mrs. Bly ordered.

Lanterns closed in around us, killing the darkness, their circles of light playing tag with each other. People were talking in low whispers and I thought I heard the deep voice of Mr. Sternlock. Did I dare stand up to ask him if he was finally satisfied? Elmer Sternlock and his damn federal government. I was fixing to do just that when something more important happened.

"Munch?"

My face was close to Hem's now, as I held both sides of his head in my hands.

"I'm right here, Hem. I won't say I forgive you, so don't ask. But I reckon we all understand how you feel about your pa, because I love mine."

As I said it, another part of my mind was remembering the Lord's Prayer, and how everyone ought to be forgiven. Even folks who hurt us. Maybe because we hurt them.

Hem spoke again, almost to the night as well as to me, his words sounding as broken as his body.

"Munch . . . promise me . . . I want you to have her, someday. You wed Blessing."

"I aim to, Hem."

"And . . . don't settle to this town. Live uproad, up on our mountain, or wherever you both belong."

Swallowing, I said, "I'm your friend again, Hem. And you're mine. Say it. Say we're pals like we always are."

Hem Lion shook his head, closing his eyes. His voice was leaving, escaping somewhere, some going-home uproad place higher than Kipp's Mountain. A sweet place. "No," he said, "you ain't my friend now."

He died, saying, "You're family."